Handling Headship

Management Books

Richard Greenfield

Published by Scholastic Publications Ltd,
Marlborough House, Holly Walk,
Leamington Spa, Warwickshire CV32 4LS

Written by Richard Greenfield
Edited by Janet Parsons
Sub-edited by Catherine Baker
Illustrated by Jane Bottomley
Front cover photograph by Martyn Chillmaid
Designed by Sue Limb

Designed using Aldus Pagemaker
Processed by Pages Bureau,
Leamington Spa
Printed and bound by Richard Clay Ltd,
Bungay, Suffolk

British Library Cataloguing in Publication Data
Greenfield, Richard
Handling headship. - (Management books).
1. Great Britain. Primary Schools. Management
I. Title
372.1200941

ISBN 0-590-76205-2

Contents

Introduction 5

Chapter One 9

Out of the frying-pan 11
Starting out 11
Setting goals 14
Your picture of the school 16
Assessing the school 18

Chapter Two 21

Building an image 23
Looking for a role model 24
Different viewpoints 25
How do you want to be seen? 27

Chapter Three 31

The headteacher and children 33
The children's view 34
Introducing new children to school 35
Continuity and progression 39
Children with special needs 39
Praise or punishment? 40

Chapter Four 41

Communication 43
Deciding on a policy 44
Establishing a communications network 45
Getting the message across 45
A two-way process 48
Being available to the staff 51

Chapter Five 53
Meetings in school 55
Ingredients for success 56
How often? 57
Who attends? 58
Preparation 59
Conducting the meeting 60
Strategies for managing meetings 62
Recording the proceedings 63
Continuity of purpose 64

Chapter Six 65
Towards a management structure 67
The traditions of primary school management 68
Management arrangements 69
Collective curriculum responsibility 71
A senior management team 73
The deputy head 74
The art of delegation 76
Appraisal 76

Chapter Seven 77
Planning the curriculum 79
The curriculum and the law 80
Achieving staff involvement 81
Monitoring and record-keeping 86
A special needs policy 86
A School Development Plan 87
Differing perspectives 88

Chapter Eight 89
Relations with the office 91
Finding out who does what 91
The role of the LEA 94
Assessing priorities 94
Getting things done 96

Chapter Nine 97
Making ends meet 99
Governors and financial delegation 100
The use of public funds under LMS 101
Planning your expenditure 104
Private funds 107

Chapter Ten 109
Working with parents 111
How do we think of parents? 111
Parents in school 113
Fund raising by parents 118
School brochure 119
Communicating with parents 120

Chapter Eleven 121
Keeping a record 123
In search of a better system 123
Reviewing the existing system 127
The key to a record-keeping system 128

Chapter Twelve 129
Day-to-day concerns 131
The school day 132
Arrangement of classes 134
Staffing arrangements 137
Directed time 138

Introduction

Introduction

At its best, headship is one of the most rewarding jobs imaginable. However, many new headteachers find themselves, with little preparation, cast into a very powerful and isolated position with few clear guidelines about what they are supposed to be doing or how best to go about the job. From the first day of their appointment in a school, headteachers are totally in charge and responsible to their governors for the organisation of the premises, finances, equipment, children and staff. They are also expected to make instant policy decisions and rulings about almost anything, and to be an authority on all things relating to the school – and quite a few things outside it as well.

Before their appointment, some headteachers will have spent hardly more than half a day in the school of which they are now in charge. Some may not even have met their predecessor, and many, especially if they take up appointments in the middle of the year, will have to manage a system they have not introduced with a staff they do not know. If we add to this confused situation the fact that newly-appointed headteachers often transfer between authorities, and that it is by no means uncommon for a new headteacher to have no deputy, it is nothing short of miraculous that after a time, headteachers usually become members of one of the most versatile, resourceful, tolerant and patient occupational groups there is.

This book, while not claiming to be a work of reference, is intended as a source of support, advice and reassurance to those taking up a headship for the first time. Others may also find the book of use. Deputies will probably one day become headteachers, and even experienced headteachers may, in these days of rapid change in education, welcome another perspective on the job they have been doing so well for so long. Those with considerable experience may feel that parts of this book are telling them things they already know. However, it is hoped that the book as a whole will bring forward some new ideas and a different viewpoint on what can be an extremely challenging and rewarding job.

Chapter One

Out of the frying-pan

Starting out

The warm glow you feel on learning that you are to be appointed headteacher of a primary school may quickly be replaced by a nagging doubt.

Of course you are the right person for the job; that's why you applied for it, and that's why the interviewing panel appointed you and not the other candidates. But how much do you really know about the school? You may have spent only a short time looking around before the interview, and meetings with children and staff may have been brief and uninformative. What is the best way to start? What should you do first and, perhaps more to the point, what should you avoid doing?

Forming impressions

The first thing you should avoid is jumping to conclusions about the school and the people who work there. You have seen it in perhaps the worst possible light. Imagine how teachers feel when a new head is being chosen. They watch the procession of hopefuls going around the school and try to guess which one is to be the new boss. They are anxious not to create the wrong impression but, human nature being what it is, this often means they come across as the exact opposites of their real selves. Self-assured, efficient people become withdrawn and reticent, while the muddlers and the inefficient appear gushing and self-confident.

The second thing to avoid is any demonstration of the self-doubt you are experiencing. Teachers in a school where there is a new head expect change, disruption and inconvenience, but they hope to be spared indecisiveness and uncertainty. If they think you lack self-confidence or don't know what you are doing, they will find it difficult to recognise you as a leader.

It's important to bear in mind that the staff are in a situation not far removed from your own. They may all feel threatened by the new regime, and all of them will be trying to weigh you up. They have seen you for only a short time, but there will already be plenty of rumours about what is going to happen once you take up the post.

Another important thing to remember when taking over is that you will be able to change some things very quickly, some things more gradually, and there are some things you will never be able to change. It helps to develop a philosophy of changing the things you can and tolerating the things you can't. This outlook, coupled with the avoidance of change for its own sake, will help you to retain your sanity in the early days.

Weighing up the situation

You can learn a great deal from your predecessor about the organisation and running of the school, even if you disagree with her approach. There are many advantages in trying to set up a briefing session with the previous incumbent before you take up your appointment.

Probably, you will already have met the headteacher in your pre-interview visit to the school. The best approach now is to telephone, re-introduce yourself, and ask how she feels about meeting to discuss your appointment. Be deferential in your attitude, and if you are invited to the school, remember to behave as any other visitor, and not as if you are already in charge.

During your meeting with the headteacher, ask:

• Would it be possible for you to come into the school to meet staff and to discuss arrangements and organisation? This can be particularly useful if the changeover occurs at the end of the school year, because many long-term decisions are made at this time and it is often difficult or impossible to change these in September. If information is exchanged at this stage, a smoother transition can be achieved than might otherwise be the case. It will also help you to feel more at home in the early days, and more involved with the organisation, simply because you have been part of the planning.

• Might it be possible for you to attend staff meetings during the term before you take up your appointment? This requires a particularly enlightened approach on the part of existing heads and governors.

• Could you arrange to have access to the school during the holidays? A few hours on your own in an empty school, armed with the keys, is worth a great deal. It will help you to assess the situation with respect to equipment, resources and organisation far better than any conducted tour. You will have a chance to look in cupboards and classrooms which you may not previously have been shown, and you will be able to form an independent impression of the school's facilities, organisation and curriculum. You can tell a great deal about a school by looking at what is on the walls and the way the classrooms are arranged.

• Where can you find important files and documents? You should read the personal files of all the staff. This will give you details of their experience and background and may enable you to form a more objective view of each individual before you see them at work. You need to know as much as you can about the school and the people who work there if you are to make reasoned judgements and sensible, informed decisions.

There is no substitute for reading yourself into the job before taking over officially. Files marked 'Letters to Parents' or 'Memos to Staff' can be particularly informative about school policy and past difficulties. Minutes of governors' meetings will provide valuable insights into the politics of the school, its pressing issues and the personalities involved. You will also be able to draw conclusions about the previous head's relationship with the governors. If the departing head is unable or unwilling to help, it is worthwhile approaching the deputy and asking some detailed questions about staffing, organisation, the premises and the curriculum. However, beware of contacting the deputy and arranging a meeting in school without the head's approval.

As a basic guide, you need at least the following information:

• A list of staff by name, with details of their responsibilities, and some brief information about their career histories.
• A simple guide to the organisation of the school. How are staff used? How are classes organised?
• General information on simple school rules and traditions, for example which areas are 'out of bounds' for children, and what is the accepted school uniform.

If you don't obtain this information, you will be starting in your new post with, at best, a very patchy picture of the current situation. You will, therefore, be at a serious disadvantage when dealing with staff, parents and children, all of whom will know what is going on far better than you do.

Remember, staff, parents and children will all assume that you know everything about the school and its organisation the moment you step inside the building, and the revelation that you don't will come as a great surprise. Of course, you should be prepared to admit when you don't know something, but your credibility will be enhanced greatly by a certain amount of background knowledge.

Sometimes, of course, there is a gap of one or two terms between the old head leaving and a new one being appointed. This leads to the strange limbo period of acting headship, which decreases the likelihood that any of the outgoing head's experience and wisdom, as applied directly to the running of the school, will be available for you to use.

Setting goals

One of the most difficult problems facing any head is the need to compromise between one's ideas and ambitions for the school and the practical possibilities inherent in the buildings, the staff, the catchment area and the budget. The extent to which aspirations and practicalities are compatible has a great bearing on the success of your appointment and the amount of job satisfaction you will achieve.

Many of us feel that challenge is a necessary part of our work. If this is so, taking over a well-run, well-organised and successful school from a popular retiring head may seem a little frustrating. However, it's clear that some people enjoy challenge more than others, and the extent of the challenge has to be measured against personal ability, experience and ambition. This is why setting goals, both before and after your appointment, is so important. Recognise the things you want to do, be aware of the things that it is unlikely you will be able to do, and draw up an action programme in order of priority.

The following examples will help you to decide on the ordering of your own priorities.

Priority list

A—Immediate
Things you cannot bear to put up with a moment longer.

B—Eventual
Things that can and will be changed in due course.

C—Possible
Things that might be changed, given time, luck and continued pressure.

D—Unlikely
Things that will probably never happen, but which it is pleasant to have at the back of your mind.

Category A
Problem: The noisy, disorganised way in which children assemble for class and are dismissed in the evening. There are implications for order and safety.

Response: You need to be clear about what you want to do. Talk to the deputy about why things are the way they are, and what you feel should be happening. Immediate changes can be introduced by 'edict'. Be clear and concise, and be prepared to justify your changes.
Problem: Haphazard and lax arrangements for playground supervision by staff.
Response: Produce a workable system which meets your requirements and present it at your first staff meeting. Give your reasons for changing the system, and do not be easily swayed by comments supporting the old system.
Problem: The practice of holding daily acts of collective worship has been allowed to lapse. Instead there are occasional events - weekly or perhaps monthly - which do not fill the requirements of the Education Reform Act.
Response: As soon as practical, inform the staff of your intention to hold acts of worship on a regular basis. Set a time for them and lead them yourself. Once the practice is re-established, you may find it possible to extend the activity and to involve staff in different ways.

Category B
Problem: Confused and badly-managed curriculum leadership. The staff have no clear ideas as to what their specific responsibilities are.
Response: This will not be solved overnight. It will require clear thinking and a sense of purpose on your part, and a series of negotiations with all staff on an individual basis.
Problem: The previous head insisted when forming the PTA that he should automatically be chairman. You feel that this is inappropriate and you sense it will lead to a conflict of interests, among other problems.
Response: Depending on the proximity of the AGM, you may be able to deal rapidly with this. Explain your views to the management committee and stress that your wish not to be chairperson does not imply any lack of support on your part. Suggest that you will attend committee meetings as often as you are available, but that the committee must elect someone else to chair proceedings. Produce a resolution for the next AGM changing the constitution. Speak in support of that motion at the meeting, and clarify your situation.
Problem: The reading/language scheme in use in the school is at least 20 years old, and most books are in bad condition.
Response: The response will depend upon your views and those of your staff, as well as the financial resources available. Despite your view of the problem as serious and immediate, you may have to live with the situation for a while in order to ensure the best solution.
Problem: The length and timing of the school day seem to you to be wrong. Although you are a primary school, the younger children leave earlier than the older ones and the lunch break seems unreasonably long.
Response: Establish exactly why these arrangements exist. Work out how long the lunch break needs to be to accommodate all the meal sittings. Once you have a proposal, put it to the staff, take account of their views and then go to the governors with a firm suggestion which you can justify both educationally and practically. With their support, and as long as parents have also been consulted about any problems which might arise from changes in finishing time, there should be no trouble in achieving change.

Problem: From your observation of the teaching staff, you have reached the conclusion that many of them have either spent too long working with the same year group or are clearly unsuited to the age range they are teaching.
Response: Any action on this will have to wait until the end of the current academic year, and you will need to employ a cautious, tactful and well-planned approach. You will have to consider the possible outcomes of any attempt at change – there is no point in enforcing your will within the school if everyone leaves in disgust.

There may be some advantage in being sure you understand fully the strengths and weaknesses of your staff. Given this, however, there is little that is not possible ultimately.
Problem: Apparently none of the staff – teaching or non-teaching – has any form of job description, and many who have 'extra responsibilities' are unclear about how these are defined.
Response: Talk to each teacher individually and elicit from them what they think they are supposed to be doing. Add to this your own views, and gradually work towards an agreed statement for each person. Use the opportunity to build responsibilities where none existed previously, and possibly to reduce them where you feel a particular person is doing more than they should.

Category C
Problem: The state of interior decoration in the school is very poor. The paint is peeling, and plaster is cracking and falling away.
Response: A letter expressing your dismay and concern to the local authority – or the governors if your school has delegated finances – will not be inappropriate, but do not raise your hopes too high.
Problem: Although your local authority has had a scheme of providing some instrumental tuition in individual schools, your particular school receives none at all, and you have been told that there is no hope of extending the list to include other schools.
Response: Don't accept this. Keep on until someone acknowledges that it is unfair, and then work on them until some provision is made. Don't worry if this is pathetically small; it will grow.

Category D
Problem: The school hall seems to you to be too small to cope with the number of children and to allow for the range of uses to which it must be put. You feel that, ideally, a new hall should be provided; or at the very least some internal walls should be demolished and restructured to provide more space.
Response: No harm in having this sort of grand project in your mind, just in case...

Your picture of the school

Before taking over, it is useful to obtain as many objective views of the school as possible. You will have heard something of what the governors and the present head think of the school, either directly or in the information which was sent out to applicants. Remember that this information is designed to attract good candidates and may not be entirely frank. Some governors, and certainly many heads, have a rosy view of their own circumstances and may not see themselves as others see them.

The staff will have another point of view, as will the parents and the Local Education Authority, but access to these views will be limited and difficult. As soon as possible, you should meet the following people:

- Some of the Local Authority's officers;
- Representatives of any parents' association;
- The chairperson of the governors;
- The deputy head.

All these people will be interested, and in some cases anxious, to hear your plans and opinion of the school, but resist the temptation to talk about this. The purpose of these meetings is to listen to as many points of view as possible, not to outline your plans and philosophies at a time when your knowledge of the facts is limited. Obviously you should avoid any situation where you might seem to be implying criticism. It is important to guard your comments very carefully at this stage.

Your perception of the school will gradually change as you gather all this information, and this will have an effect on your approach to the headship. The knowledge which you gather may not alter your ideals, but it may have an influence on your priorities or the timing of your decisions.

Reading the signs

Before you take up your appointment, or in the few weeks after you start, look out for warning signs which may suggest that all is not well in certain areas. If you recognise these signs early on, and are prepared to deal with the problems rapidly, you may be able to use the situation to your advantage.

Some of the most frequent warning signs are:

- A lack of any formal staff consultation process;
- Evidence of parental disaffection;
- A deputy with apparently little knowledge of the workings of the school;
- Teachers who have become very rigid and set in their ways and who have spent many years working with the same year group;
- A lack of clearly defined management structure;
- A serious lack of key resources.

Evidence of significant problems will alert you to the need to take urgent action, and help you with your list of priorities.

The view you form of the school at this stage will be the result of your own professional assessment, based on your experience, and taking into account the opinions, criticism and praise of others. Many people, it should be remembered, may have ulterior motives for making things seem better or worse than they really are. You will need time to sort through all this varying information from so many different sources, and to reach your own opinion. This means you will be unwilling to make any hasty judgements or to introduce changes and developments too rapidly.

It may in fact be to your advantage to delay your decisions a little, for the effect on others of introducing a policy change too quickly can be worse than that of reserving judgement until you have command of all the facts. It is an even greater problem, of course, if you later have to reverse your decision in the light of further consideration. No one really minds having to wait a while for a decision providing that, when it is eventually made, it turns out to be the right one.

Assessing the school

When carrying out your assessment of the school, it is a good idea to consider its various aspects under the separate headings of staff, premises, curriculum and administration. Naturally there will be some overlap, but in the early days it is prudent to try to isolate your areas of concern.

Staff

Many heads find that their most immediate concern on taking up a post is the people they have to work with. The staff, both teaching and non-teaching, can have a major effect on whether you consider your early days to have been successful. Are they friendly and welcoming, or cold and withdrawn? Are they united or isolated? Are they helpful and co-operative, or apparently resentful of the newcomer?

It is unlikely that they will all take the same view, and you should set about weighing up the individuals and loosely categorising them. Remember, however, that first impressions are not always correct. Also, avoid any tendency to ally yourself with one or two members of staff who seem particularly helpful or receptive, in case you appear to be developing favourites. Make strenuous efforts to cultivate the staff with whom you feel you are having difficulties.

Add to your observations the factual information you have already obtained about the age, experience, interests and backgrounds of the staff. Once you have had the chance to supplement this with your own professional judgement of their abilities both in and out of the classroom, you will be ready to initiate your longer-term planning and staff management. The speed with which you carry this out will be determined, among other things, by the time of year at which you start your appointment. If you are forced to plan for September less than a term ahead, you will be in a hurry. If you have most of the year, you can deliberate more slowly.

It is inevitable that you will like some of your colleagues better than others. However, you must try to retain a degree of professional detachment, at least until you have established yourself more fully. You still have to work with the staff, manage them and support their professional development whether you like them or not and whether or not they seem to like you, and this can be a difficult thing to come to terms with. If you find you like all the people you have to work with, then you are indeed fortunate.

Premises

While you are expected to like all the staff, or at least to get on with them, the same is not true of the buildings.

If you are faced with a school building which is less than ideal, and want to make changes to improve the accommodation it offers, remember that to make even a small change in the fabric of a building costs a great deal. There are ways and means of making improvements, but it is often simpler to adapt your ideas to suit the building than the other way round. This may sound defeatist, but you can avoid a great deal of frustration if you set realistic and modest targets as far as the adaptation of school premises is concerned.

The school buildings may contribute greatly to the 'hidden curriculum'. The reasons why certain organisational arrangements exist often have their origins in the limitations of the building.

If a school has been built as open-plan, this will be important in determining the policy with regard to teaching style and the use of resources. If the school is on a split site or has inadequate hall accommodation, this determines the extent to which co-operative teaching is feasible, and may limit the space for PE or movement classes. If the school has excess accommodation, you have the opportunity to establish libraries, resource rooms, music rooms and so on. If the school is small and crowded, the chances of small group work are severely limited.

Your ambitions as a headteacher will have to be tempered by the limitations of the building. It is useful to do some sort of initial assessment of the site when looking at the school prior to interview to see the extent to which its potential matches your ambitions. The building is the one thing you may find it almost impossible to change.

The curriculum

Changing, developing, broadening or updating the curriculum of a school is the aspect of their job which many headteachers see as the most significant,and the nearest to the role for which their training and experience have prepared them. The curriculum is, more than anything else, the key to a successful school.

Despite the requirements of the National Curriculum, what is taught and how it is taught is still very much a matter for the headteacher, in consultation with the governors. Your own views will be a result of your training, experience and personal preferences, but you will need to adapt them, initially at least, to cover any shortcomings of the staff and the building. Nevertheless, there is little that can't be done; your main problem will be recognising your own limitations and the need to approach matters in a steady, systematic way. The temptation to try to do everything in the first half-term is great. The pressure from others for rapid development may seem just as great, but you must resist it.

Planning the curriculum requires a great deal of careful deliberation and preparation. You must be sure of your objectives and the methods by which you will meet them, as well as the resources you will need and the time-scale to which you are working. You also need to be sure that your staff are behind you.

The success of a curriculum plan depends on the governors, staff, buildings and finances, and the plan must be shaped with all these things in mind. However, success depends above all on the professional commitment, experience and knowledge of the headteacher. If these are missing, or if the headteacher is not fully convinced that what is proposed is right, then there is no chance of a curriculum plan succeeding.

In the early days of your headship, there may be pressure from outside agencies – HMI, LEA advisers, publishers and educationists – to implement reforms in the teaching of certain subjects. Bear in mind that even though they might emanate from the highest and most reputable sources, only some of these proposals are likely to be well-founded and based on successful experience. Some will be thoroughly beneficial, some will be well-intentioned but ill-advised, some will be misguided and, occasionally, some will be totally loony.

You are the experienced professional who is ultimately responsible to the governors for what goes on in school, so *you* must judge into which category each new idea falls. When doing this, remember the remarkable reforms that have occurred in primary education over the last thirty years, which owe much of their success to the foresight and willingness of the headteachers who allowed such innovations into their schools. Remember, too, the casualties — ITA, Primary French, Colour Factor and so on — which have come and gone at great expense and inconvenience to those involved. Innovations like these may have contributed to the undermining of public confidence in the teaching profession.

Administration

During your early days in school, administrative procedures, that is, how the school runs on a day-to-day basis, will probably have the greatest impact on you. Although not nearly as important in the long run as staff development, the curriculum or the premises, administration is a significant matter and one which is of immediate concern. Poor curriculum design or staff problems can be camouflaged from the casual observer quite easily; poor administration and organisation cannot be hidden. It is essential that you understand the system, are aware of its shortcomings and are able and willing to introduce your own programme to overcome these.

As an interested professional you should have formed an opinion of the school's administration and organisation on your first visit. Was your arrival expected? How were you received? Did the school present an image of efficiency or muddle? Do the people who work in the school seem to know what is going on? Is there a system or do things seem to happen in a haphazard manner? The answers to these questions play a large part in determining the view outsiders form of the school.

You will have your own views about the relative importance of administration, but you cannot overlook its significance at a superficial level. In many ways administrative changes are the easiest to implement; they are easily justified in terms of efficiency or economy, and their benefits are rapidly felt. Furthermore, they allow you to make an early impression on your colleagues in a fairly benign manner, without venturing too far along the road of radical change.

If you start from this point, you may find that the developments you propose in other areas are more readily accepted because of your modest successes here. Instigating administrative changes is one fairly risk-free way of developing the skill and confidence you need to progress to more important matters. You will be testing the staff's responses to change, assessing the level of their co-operation and, perhaps most importantly, finding out at first hand how the school can best be run.

Always remember that, although you are the professional and the person on the spot, the governors have widespread powers and responsibilities. They should be involved in proposals for change and review at every stage.

Chapter Two

Building an image

A Local Authority inspector was once paying a visit to the school of a very experienced and somewhat formidable headteacher who was on the point of retirement. Arriving at the school, the inspector was directed by the secretary to the head's room, where he found the door firmly shut. Outside the door was one of those traffic-light devices consisting of a red, a yellow and a green light, which glowed according to whether or not the head was willing to receive visitors. Each light bore a message; 'engaged', 'wait', or 'enter.'

The inspector had seen these signals before, in other schools, but as he was about to knock, something caught his eye. The printed message on the red light had been scratched out and replaced by something written in felt-tipped pen. It had clearly been done some time ago, because the writing was rather faded, but it was possible to discern two words. I leave it to your imagination what they were.

Quite how long the headteacher had been turning away hopeful visitors in this abrupt fashion was never discovered, but it was quite clear both that the head was entirely unaware of the graffito and, more interestingly, that no one had bothered to tell him about it.

How much thought do most headteachers give to the image they project to others – to their staff, to parents, to the pupils, to visitors? How do others see the school?

There is much to be said for trying to see ourselves as others see us. What we think of as brisk and efficient might be taken by some to be cold and clinical. What we imagine is informal, cosy and friendly might be interpreted as muddled and disorganised. Occasional self-examination and analysis is a worthwhile practice among teachers in general and headteachers in particular.

Looking for a role model

It is a good idea for headteachers, throughout their careers, to give conscious thought to the idea of image-building. Some people, of course, would find this an absurd point of view. Heads, like other teachers, are in the business of education and of providing the best opportunities for the children in their care. What case can there be for any notion of image-building, even assuming anyone had the time?

Let's first of all make clear what is meant by building an image. Across the country, in primary schools of all shapes and sizes, the headteachers are all carrying out the same basic job, but they are using a variety of approaches to achieve the same ends. One of the strengths of primary education in this country has been the degree of independence allowed to heads and the wide range of approaches to teaching, learning and management that have resulted.

If you could assemble two dozen primary headteachers in a room, you would find few similarities between them. Each headteacher possesses a unique and personal blend of character and ability, with styles and approaches developed through interaction over the years with numerous teachers, headteachers and others concerned with education.

The range of different types of headteacher makes it difficult for a prospective head to choose one particular individual as the ideal type to emulate. It must also be accepted that what works for one person seldom works for another in the same way or to the same extent.

The same principle applies in teaching. As students we may have seen particular teachers working in certain ways and having great success, but may have had disastrous results when we tried the same approach. This is due partly to lack of experience and skill, but partly to something else as well. Each personality interacts uniquely with others, so that great variations in response arise.

Clearly, then, we each have to approach the role of headteacher in ways which we find successful and enjoyable. An awareness of the types of approach available and an understanding of which ones are most suited to us is part of the process of image-building as a headteacher. The development of this awareness is important for success as a headteacher.

Image-building does not mean comparing types in a critical sense, or even implying that one style is better than any other. If the end result is a successful, happy school, that is all that matters. However, you need to be aware of the alternatives, at least in the early days of headship, and to allow yourself a chance to arrive at a decision about the best approach to use.

Different viewpoints

The idea of image is relevant to headteachers in a number of ways. It applies to the ways we as headteachers see our job, and to the way visitors see us and our role. It is important in our relationship with the others who work in the school, including of course the children. Finally, it is vital to have an awareness of our image in relation to outside agencies, such as the governors and the Local Authority.

One of the criticisms of proposals for the appraisal of headteachers was that it would be difficult to find anyone with a sufficiently objective view of the school and the headteacher who also had appropriate knowledge of the way in which the headteacher carried out the job.

The headteacher of any school is seen in a different way by each of the numerous people he or she has to deal with in the course of his or her work. Let's consider the range of factors which may influence the view taken of the headteacher by a variety of people.

The staff

The staff's view of the headteacher will be coloured by the way in which he or she deals with the immediate day-to-day process of running a school. Is class cover always arranged? Is the communication network good? Are resources freely available?

A lot of these considerations are superficial and fail to take into account the more profound aspects of running a school, but to those who work in a school, they are frequently the most important issues.

At another level, teachers will be looking for a headteacher who supports them and offers them help and guidance when they feel they need it. They also look for someone who gives them the chance of satisfactory professional development by considering their needs and aspirations and by making INSET available.

The parents

The parents may want to see someone who obviously knows what is going on in all the classrooms, who appears to have direct personal knowledge of their child, who is available at short notice at any time of day to discuss their problems, no matter how trivial, and who runs a well-disciplined and well-organised school. Above all, parents seem to want a high-profile headteacher, and tend to take a short- to medium-term view of school organisation.

The pupils

The pupils' view of the headteacher is perhaps the most significant. It deserves particular attention, and is the subject of Chapter 3.

The governors

The view of most governors is rather more distant than that of pupils, parents or staff. Although governors are being forced to become more and more involved in the day-to-day activities of their schools with the increase in their legal responsibilities, they are still one or two places removed from the immediacy of the school which staff, pupils and parents experience.

Governors will, by and large, tend to take a longer-term view of what is going on. They will be pleased if they are not inundated by complaints about the headteacher and staff, and will hope to see things going on in a smooth, unruffled way.

They will be concerned to have an overview of the proceedings. For many governors, an ideal head is one who runs a successful school, and who also keeps them informed. Governors often appreciate an opportunity to become more involved in the school, and would like the headteacher to make them aware of curriculum developments, without being patronising. They do, after all, need to make decisions in consultation with the headteacher and staff.

The relationship between the headteacher and his or her governors is often the most complicated and difficult to handle.

The Local Authority

The Local Authority will have an even more distant view of the school than the governors, and will therefore have a different set of criteria for a good headteacher.

Firstly, they will be anxious that the headteacher runs an effective school, in their terms, and keeps their involvement to a minimum. To them, complaints and referrals are bad news, so in this sense the less they hear about a particular school the better.

Secondly, they will be anxious that the headteacher responds rapidly and co-operatively to their initiatives, and that she complies with the various administrative requirements within the prescribed deadlines.

Other viewpoints

So far we have looked at the image of the headteacher from the point of view of the staff, the pupils, the parents, the governors and the Local Authority. Although these are the main groups you need to be concerned with, there are many smaller groups, each with their own priorities and their own criteria for a good headteacher.

Some headteachers, for instance, may have a relationship with the community they serve outside the immediate context of the parents. There may be ethnic minority groups to consider. The head-teachers of church schools have to relate to the Diocesan Authorities. Heads who share a site with another school have to be mindful of the image they project to the headteacher of this school.

As a headteacher, you may or may not be concerned about your image in relation to other headteachers. Are you receptive to advice? Do you offer advice if approached? Do you engage in partnership schemes or joint ventures?

Thinking about all this it may well seem that, in order to succeed as a head-teacher, you have to be all things to all people. This often seems to be the case, but there are also some other factors to bear in mind.

The first important point to remember is that it is not possible to be an effective headteacher, or indeed a leader of any kind, if your aim is to keep everyone happy. The nature of headship involves the risk, and the necessity on occasions, that you will be unpopular with one or

other of the groups to which you have to relate. The skill lies in ensuring, by your actions, that this situation remains fluid; you should offset unpopularity in one area with popularity in another in an ever-changing, dynamic equilibrium.

How do you want to be seen?

If your idea of a desirable image for a headteacher is that of a popular, benevolent figure, you are likely to run into difficulties fairly early on. You will have learned in the classroom that the kind, smiling teacher who gives away everything on the first day of term and keeps nothing in reserve can run into trouble by Christmas. It is just the same for a headteacher.

Although headteachers have to possess good all-round skills, the headteacher who sets out to prove to everyone that he is capable of doing every job in the school may not achieve as much success and respect as the one who recognises his own strengths and weaknesses and adjusts his work-load accordingly.

If, as a headteacher, you wish to create the image of being a competent teacher, capable and confident with all age groups and able to lead from the front in the various areas of practice, you must realise that, although there is much to be said for this approach, particularly in terms of the way the staff view you, there are also drawbacks. This is especially true if you plan to commit yourself to a substantial teaching timetable. In this case you may find that your availability to others and your ability to cope with the pressures of administration and planning will be compromised.

If, on the other hand, you see yourself primarily in a counselling or consultancy role, available to staff, children and parents, the need to be routinely available may limit the time and energy you have to spare for other aspects of your role as headteacher.

There is a wide, indeed almost infinite range of approaches which the headteacher can take, and this is something you need to consider carefully.

Availability and approachability

There are many things that can affect the image of the headteacher as perceived by the people he or she works with, both in and out of school.

Headteachers frequently surround themselves with an extensive protective barrier which must deter many would-be visitors and convey the wrong message to many others.

Try putting yourself in the position of a visitor to the school — perhaps a prospective parent, a Local Authority officer or someone else with business to undertake - and try to see what impression the school makes and what welcome is offered.

The appointment system, the over-protective secretary, the closed door, all convey a message of unapproachability and a lack of welcome. Why are all these things thought necessary, and what more acceptable alternatives might be considered?

The appointment system

There is a sound reason for structuring the working day on an appointment system. Headteachers need to plan their time, and this is not practical if visitors are encouraged to turn up casually and unannounced. Making an advance arrangement is courteous, and is also a matter of common sense. However, the nature of schools means that there will be times when prior warning is not possible. The system must allow for a parent to turn up on the off-chance with an urgent problem.

If you have a widely publicised policy of expecting visitors to make appointments, except in cases of emergency, there should be no need for off-putting notices or other deterrents.

The closed door

It can be a good idea to do away with the closed door policy. Make it widely known that if your office door is open and you are in there, any of the staff are free to come and talk to you about anything. If the door is closed, then you do not wish to be disturbed. This is a fairly straightforward policy which, in the main, avoids misunderstanding and embarrassment.

The secretary

Once a visitor has arrived to see you, how is he received? Is he taken by the secretary to your room, shown in and introduced? Is he sent along and told to knock on the door? Do you come out, introduce yourself in the secretary's office and then take the visitor back with you to your own office?

Each one of these approaches is widely used, not only in schools but also in doctors' surgeries, banks, solicitors' offices and a whole range of other enterprises. The particular approach you adopt says much about the image you want to create, and about your own self-image.

Of the three approaches described, the last one is perhaps the best. To many people the prospect of approaching and knocking on a strange door, and then entering an unfamiliar room, there perhaps to meet a stranger seated behind a desk, can be daunting. Even if the experience is tempered by the company of the secretary, it can still be overwhelming. How much better to be allowed a short while to compose yourself in a general office or waiting-room and then to be welcomed by the person you have come to meet.

The headteacher needs protection from casual and unsolicited or unwelcome callers, and must have the possibility of working undisturbed if necessary. This provision has to be made without making the school an unwelcoming place which requires nerves of steel to enter. This is not to suggest that you should move your desk into the front entrance and be available constantly to all callers. You need to assess the situation with a mixture of compromise, balance and common sense.

Self-assessment

Even when the visitor is safely inside your office, there may still be barriers to overcome. Do you sit behind a desk carefully placed between yourself and the visitor? Does the visitor sit in a hard, upright chair while you lounge in an upholstered armchair? Allowing for the fact that a considerable number of headteachers up and down the country still have no office of their own, you should ask yourself what message you are conveying by the way your office is furnished and the furniture arranged.

- Where is your desk situated? Does it form a barrier to visitors?
- What sort of chairs are available for visitors?
- Can you create a relaxed atmosphere, using easy chairs and a coffee table for more informal discussion, or is it always assumed that you will remain behind the desk like a doctor confronting a patient?

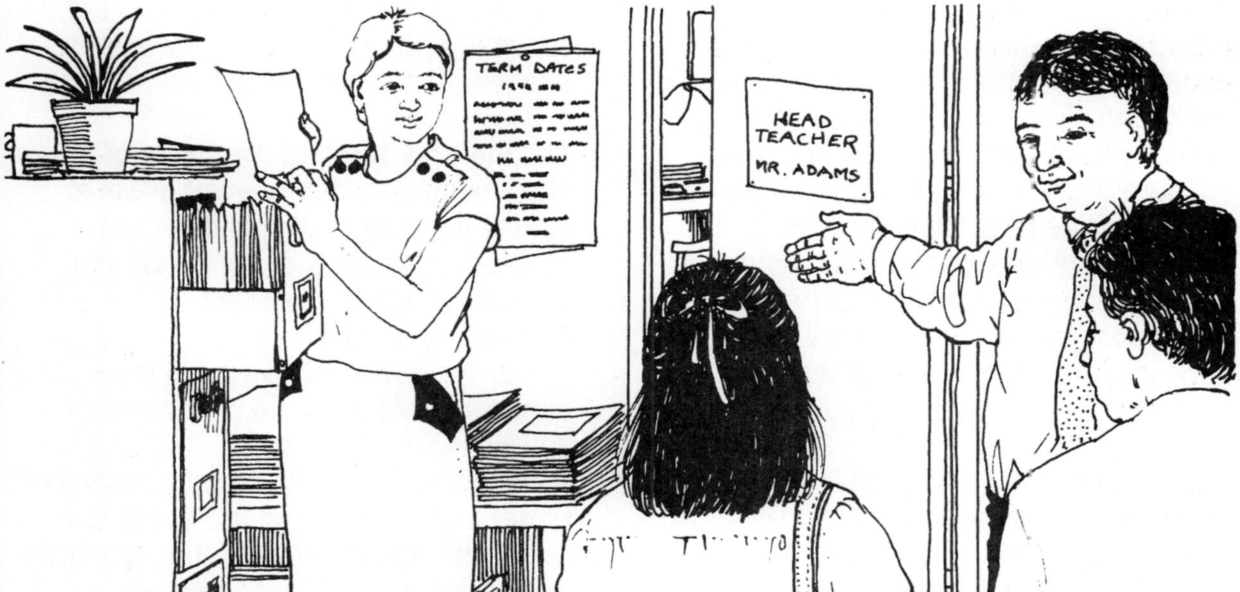

• Once you have a visitor, how effective is your system of advising others that you are busy and do not wish to be disturbed?
• Can you divert telephone calls?
• If necessary and appropriate, can you provide visitors with tea or coffee without a major disturbance and without disrupting the secretary's work?

It may be a useful exercise to extend this form of self-analysis to other areas of your activities throughout the school. You could use the same questioning approach in considering your use of the staffroom, the degree of involvement you choose to have with the children, or the way you interact with other staff and parents at meetings.

Without spending too long trying to explain the significance of particular actions, you should be aware of a possible dichotomy between your intentions and the way they are interpreted. To avoid this you require, firstly, a clear understanding of your own motives and the image you are trying to project and, secondly, some comprehension of the way you and your actions appear to the many different people your job requires you to come in contact with. This is no easy task, but success in this area will lead to a more effective and satisfying form of headship.

Setting the tone of the school

The headteacher is vitally important in setting the tone of the school, from children's standards of behaviour and attitudes to work to policies on multicultural relations.

You should have considered the atmosphere of the school before your application, to make sure it felt comfortable. However, once in post, don't forget that your own attitudes and standards will be reflected throughout the school. You should have your own carefully considered viewpoints on important subjects, which will then be transmitted naturally, in the course of day-to-day activities, to those around you.

Chapter Three

The headteacher and children

With all the pressures on headteachers to become managers, administrators, accountants, PR experts and communicators, it would be easy to lose sight of the fact that headteachers are principally responsible for the welfare and education of the children in their care. There is no escaping the fact that the best schools are those in which the well-being and education of the children naturally take precedence over all other considerations and concerns.

There is plenty of demand for headteachers who are dedicated to the welfare and education of children, and who have a flair for management. There should be no place in education for managers who who see the children as incidental to the process.

This chapter looks at various aspects of a headteacher's relationship with the children in the school, and gives some guidelines for developing and improving it. There is also some advice on handling the induction of children into the school, including such matters as the sort of information that should be supplied to prospective parents.

The children's view

Shortly after I had been appointed to my first headship, I was in my office one afternoon, just after the end of school, trying to make some sense of the job I found myself doing. The office faced on to a pathway which led from the main door to the gate, and the large window had been thoughtfully provided with net curtains. Two of the very youngest children were walking slowly by, and when they reached my window, they stopped and busied themselves trying to peer through the net. Fascinated by this, I listened to their conversation.

'What's in there?' enquired one.

'That's the headteacher's office,' replied the other knowingly.

'What does he do?'

I waited anxiously for the reply.

'He tells you off,' came the chastening response.

These children's perception of the role of the headteacher was clear. Although I had not been at the school long enough for them to have had much first hand experience of me, they saw the headteacher as someone whose role was essentially punitive and critical.

On many occasions since then, the image of the headteacher as someone who is placed in a school to tell other people off has returned to me. Is this image justified? In how many schools throughout the country would you find, especially during lunchtime, little knots of children waiting in the corridor outside the headteacher's room, having been sent there by teachers or supervisors for some kind of ultimate sanction?

Sadly it is no doubt true that, in many cases, increasing administrative demands have led to the headteacher becoming distanced from the children. It is quite common these days, at least in larger primary schools, for the headteacher to have no regular teaching commitment. The only contact some children have with their headteacher is on the odd occasions when he has to cover classes in the absence of other teachers.

When parents have complaints relating to the school, they usually take them to the headteacher. Children frequently overhear the criticisms and comments made at home, and these may seem to them to associate the headteacher with the difficulties being experienced. If, as often happens, the children's only contact with the headteacher is when they are in trouble or when there are problems, it is hardly surprising if the basic general perceptions they form of this figure-head are negative.

There are a number of ways in which you can help children to form a more positive view of their headteacher. The following ideas may be of help to you when considering this matter:

- Try to learn the name of each child in the school (of course, this may be impossible if your school is on the large side).
- Be seen around the school as much as possible. Take your turn in the dining-room and playground, and wander in and out of classrooms now and then, stopping to chat to children and teachers if appropriate.
- *Don't* expect everyone to stop work and greet you formally when you enter a classroom. If you want to talk to the children as a group, make a point of asking their teacher beforehand if he minds you doing so.

• Involve yourself with the children. Use your talents: join in with sports or musical activities.
• Wait at the gate or school entrance before and after school, to greet and chat to children and parents.

Introducing new children to school

In recent years many schools have been giving careful thought to the ways in which they introduce children to life at school. This induction process is seen as vitally important in settling children rapidly into the school routine, so that they can progress more quickly in learning during their early years.

There are many aspects which can go to make up a successful induction process, but they will not all work equally well in every school. In general, though, the aims of any induction process should be as follows:

• To find out as much relevant information as possible about the children before they begin school;
• To give parents as much information about the school as possible, and to offer advice on the best ways they can start preparing their children for school;
• To give the children some experience of school and the chance to meet some of those who work there;
• To encourage a dialogue between parents and school staff. In talking with parents, teachers will have a chance to alleviate any worries about the prospect of children starting school. Clear and direct communication between staff and parents will also reduce the chances of misunderstandings occurring.

The way in which these aims will be achieved will vary according to the individual school, headteacher and staff, but the following activities should help you to introduce or review an induction programme in your own school.

Registering children

The ways in which children are registered for school vary from area to area. The importance placed on this process depends on the policy of the local authority and the school itself, the number of applications, the likelihood of over-subscription and the nature of the community the school serves. There are, however, a number of common features.

Nowadays parents are often encouraged to visit schools, either at the time they register their child or before registration, in order to help them make a choice of school. The way in which they are received and the type of information they are given will affect parents' opinions of a school permanently for good or ill. It is therefore clearly very important to present the school as well as possible.

Prospective parents should be given the opportunity to look around the school while the children are at work. You could organise a 'conducted tour'; this can be time-consuming, but if it becomes standard practice it will become more straightforward both for you and for the teachers who are being 'looked at'.

School literature

It is a legal requirement for schools to publish certain information about themselves, and a school brochure can be a good way of conveying to prospective parents something of the aims of the school. The subject of school literature is dealt with at greater length in Chapter 10; see page 119.

Home visits

A useful way of building a relationship between home and school is through home visits. Although expensive in terms of manpower, these are a valuable exercise. Naturally the school cannot insist on the parent's co-operation, but it is rare to find any unwillingness, especially once the process is established as part of the induction programme. You should of course take care to explain the purpose of the visits beforehand.

One of the staff who will have regular contact with the children during their first year in school — usually the teacher, but possibly a nursery nurse — should arrange to visit the children's homes before the start of term.

Staff may have reservations about undertaking such visits, but these will vanish once the benefits become clear.

The format of home visits needs to be planned carefully to ensure maximum value to all concerned. You should make sure that the visits offer the following:

- A chance for the teacher to find out the sort of information which could not be included in the more straightforward form of application;
- An informal opportunity for the parents to ask detailed questions about starting school in general and the chosen school in particular;
- Time for the teacher to offer practical advice about ways in which the parents can prepare their children for school;
- Finally, and perhaps most importantly, a chance for the child to meet one of the people who is to be a significant figure in her school life.

The information obtained from the visit should be limited to that which is likely to be of value in the coming year. This information must then be stored in such a way that it is readily available to those who will be professionally involved with the children.

Information sheets

Whether or not you decide to adopt the practice of home visits, it is useful to give parents an information sheet in the term before their children start school. This should outline the following points, less formally than the school booklet:

- The day-to-day routines of school;
- What children may wear and bring with them;
- The session times;
- The people to contact about worries;
- A summary of rules and procedures.

You could also offer reassurance about starting school and give some guidance on preparing children for this big step. The aim is to build a relationship with the parents by answering queries, allaying worries and giving information.

Preparatory visits to school

It is fairly common these days for children to visit their new school before they start formally. The form of such visits should be carefully thought out.

The main purpose of the visit is to give the child a chance to see the classroom she is going to be working in, and to meet the teacher and, if possible, some classmates. Ideally this would be achieved by removing the existing class of children and ensuring that only small numbers of visiting children attend at each session. The children should be separated from their parents for at least some of the time, both to get them used to the idea and to enable staff to spot potential problems in this respect. Meeting the parents on their own gives you the chance to give them more information about the school, and to invite further questions. The more chances you have to do this the better.

The staff can use classroom visits as an opportunity to carry out some limited informal assessment of each child. If the class teacher is free from the responsibility of the normal class and can concentrate on the small group of visiting children, he or she will be able to devote time to making informal assessments and spotting any possible problems. It is a good idea for children to be engaged in a range of simple activities — colouring, sorting, playing with bricks, sand or water. The teacher can then see fairly quickly which children have reached particular stages of development. A few simple notes made at this stage can save a lot of time at the beginning of term.

Other visits

Before starting school, many children have attended nursery units or playgroups. It is valuable for the teachers who will be working with the reception class to visit these to observe the children and talk with the staff. The children will also get to know their new teacher, in a limited sense at least.

The possibility of such liaison depends, of course, upon the number of playgroups and nurseries which feed your school. It can be useful to build a relationship with the principal ones. Inviting their staff to visit and spend some time in your reception classes can help enormously in establishing a relationship.

Continuity and progression

One of the principal responsibilities of a headteacher is to ensure that each child in the school is provided with learning objectives and opportunities which will enable him or her to:

- Make sense of the world in which he or she lives;
- Express ideas and thoughts through language, mathematics, science, art and the other areas of the curriculum.

The National Curriculum has provided a framework within which headteachers can execute at least part of this responsibility, but there is still a need to assess, monitor and record, and to identify the special needs of particular children. No headteacher can do this alone.

The headteacher, as manager, must create and maintain an environment in which appropriate learning is possible. The headteacher's leadership and delegation should enable the staff to carry out effectively the various functions imposed on them by the curriculum.

Policies in this respect need to be clear and workable, but you must never lose sight of the fact that they relate to the children. The individual should never be overlooked in the interests of the establishment as a whole.

The progress of a child through school involves a lot more than academic achievement. You must also be concerned with the child's social welfare, with pastoral care and with other aspects of a child's development which cannot be measured by attainment targets. Your job is to ensure, through a combination of leadership, management and delegation, that these aspects are not overlooked. They must be given a prominent place in any consideration of progress and continuity.

This is a demanding task and one which can be overshadowed by the administrative and academic pressures placed on headteachers by modern practices. Schools which emphasise these aspects tend to be regarded as 'caring schools'. There is, sadly, an element of criticism of this ideal. Among some groups the notion of caring is synonymous with a lowering of standards or a reduction in efficiency. There is no reason why this view should be accepted or even tolerated; it is perfectly possible to lead a school which is caring, efficient *and* capable of high standards of achievement.

Children with special needs

Purists might say that all children have special educational needs because they are all unique, and each child must be treated as an individual. The headteacher has to ensure that the unique qualities of each child are recognised and his or her potential developed. However, some children exhibit specific characteristics or problems which make the job of the headteacher and staff more demanding.

You have a responsibility to ensure that the school operates a policy which allows children with special needs to be identified, assessed, monitored and integrated where possible into normal activities. The following check-list might help you to introduce or review a special needs policy.

Special needs check-list

- Does your school have a special needs policy of which all staff are aware?
- What facilities exist for identifying and reporting learning and behavioural difficulties among children?
- Is there a teacher designated as special needs co-ordinator?
- Does the special needs co-ordinator have a job description?
- Does the special needs co-ordinator have sufficient non-contact time to enable him or her to undertake the job properly?
- Is there a procedure for monitoring and reviewing the cases of individual children?
- Have you established an efficient liaison network with outside agencies?
- How do you inform parents of problems, difficulties, worries and special programmes of work?
- What arrangements are there for the provision of special work programmes?

Praise or punishment?

In many children's eyes a visit to the headteacher is linked with the idea of punishment or criticism. This idea is reinforced by the headteachers in literature, by the expectations and experiences of parents and, in some cases, by the children's own experiences of headteachers.

The headteacher's role does, of course, include giving teachers support in respect of control and discipline. Most headteachers recognise that teaching staff occasionally reach a point when they no longer feel capable of dealing with a particular situation within the classroom, and may then refer a child or group of children to the headteacher. This is a situation which calls for tact, sympathy and understanding.

Some people would say that the teacher is demonstrating a failure by this action, and further weakening the relationship with the child or children concerned. More importantly, others consider this course of action damaging to the notion of a team approach to the problem, implying an inability on the part of one teacher to deal with the matter, and a superiority on the part of the head.

Faced with this situation, you should avoid the pitfall of being seen to punish children simply because they have been sent to you. Try to hear each child's own version of events and that of anyone else involved, including the teacher. The difficulty is that you may seem to be setting yourself up as judge, and there is a possibility that you may not agree with the teacher's decision. The effects of such an apparent lack of trust in the teacher's judgement can be serious, and you need to be aware of this.

Ultimately, you should always be seen to support the teacher's judgements. Any disagreements should be settled quietly. If you disagree with a teacher's referral of a child, you can reflect this openly in dealing with the child – for example giving him no further punishment – and discreetly in discussion with the teacher afterwards.

Some headteachers make it known to their staff that there is no question of children being referred to them, and that matters must be sorted out by the teachers concerned. This approach is unrealistic and unsupportive. Far better, if you feel this way, to develop some system of pastoral support within the school, involving other staff, which can be called upon if a teacher has difficulties.

Chapter Four

Communication

Good all-round communication is one of the keys to so much that is enviable and desirable in a well-run primary school. You can run a school with minimal communication, but you can't run a good school, and you can't run a happy school.

When people think about problems of communication in schools they usually imagine the difficulties arising in large establishments with hundreds of children, many staff and perhaps a split site. It seems almost impossible that a tiny community of two, three or four teachers can lack communication, but this is often the case.

Because of the anticipated problems with communication, larger schools often have elaborate systems which serve to inform everyone in a reasonably efficient way. In small schools it is often the very fact that everyone works so closely together which causes problems; one tends to assume that the others all know about everything that is going on.

Deciding on a policy

As a headteacher you will need to decide on the way you will disseminate information within the school, and particularly among the staff. Do you intend to operate a closed system in which normally no one is told anything that they do not need to know, or would you rather have an open system whereby everyone is told everything that is not obviously private and confidential?

The first of these approaches is much less time-consuming than the second, and it also has the advantage that accidental indiscretions are unlikely to occur. Sometimes it can also be a useful system to operate if you wish to use internal staffroom politics by keeping some staff informed of a particular matter while leaving others in the dark.

The second system, while requiring more effort and time, has the advantage of reducing suspicion among members of staff that they are not being told everything. Once a policy of open management is recognised and accepted, people will become more willing to share information among themselves and to discuss their problems and difficulties with colleagues. However, care has to be taken when using this system that confidentiality is maintained where appropriate, as otherwise staff will feel they cannot raise matters with you in confidence.

When reviewing the organisation of the school you should pay special attention to the network of communication. 'Nobody told me!' is a common cry in many schools, and every headteacher should try as hard as possible to prevent it being heard.

There are a number of reasons why teachers plead ignorance. Some are the fault of the system, some the fault of the headteacher and some the fault of the staff. Beware of assuming that because you know or understand something, then everyone in the school knows or understands it as well. If something needs to be made clear, you have a duty to ensure that everyone knows about it, including the teacher who was out on playground duty when you went into the staffroom and told everyone else.

To reduce the risk of giving rise to misunderstandings it is important to have an agreed and understood policy on communication. Your policy should aim to make things as simple as possible, and should ideally work on a default system, whereby if you don't hear of a change in, say, the time or date set for a meeting, it is safe to assume that the first message you got about it was correct.

Communication in planning

One of the secrets of good communication is good planning. If staff have ample advance notice of important dates and events throughout the year, they should only need to be told if it is necessary to change these dates; this is the default system in action. If the practice is established whereby the dates for staff meetings are determined at the first meeting of the year, no one has an excuse for not knowing the dates, providing that they were present.

The more established the practice of long-term planning becomes, the easier it is to fit into the structure of organisation within the school, and the more effective it is as a way of ensuring that everyone knows what is going on.

Establishing a communications network

Although most of us talk much more than we write, verbal communication is often less effective at getting a message across than writing. There are various potential problems and traps. If you have to tell everyone something and you choose to do it verbally, you have to remember whom you have and haven't told. You have to ensure that each person is listening, that they understand what you are saying, and that everyone gets the same message. Remember also that someone who has forgotten to do what you asked may deny that you ever told them in the first place.

In most cases, of course, verbal communication is quite satisfactory in a day-to-day working relationship. You will have to judge the occasions on which more formal methods are needed. If a routine is established for the delivery of information, staff will come to recognise that certain messages are more important than others, and will react to them accordingly.

The ideal is to build up a communications network which takes account of your own weaknesses and those of your staff, and which offers the greatest opportunity for everyone to know everything that is going on in the school, without any breaches of confidence. At the same time the relative importance of the messages needs to be made clear; the important ones should stand out among the wealth of less significant information.

Building up such a system takes time, and will involve many trials and errors. If something clearly is not working, give it up and try something else, but don't be afraid to re-introduce the same system at a later date if things have changed.

Getting the message across

What follows is a list of ideas which may offer some help in building a successful and efficient communications network in your school. Remember, there is no substitute for talking to people, but you do need substantial back-up.

Choose items from the list below and use them selectively to suit your own circumstances. If you use them all, you and your staff will have to work very hard, but you will have a good communications network.

Diaries

Issue all your staff with school year diaries and make updating them with future events a routine part of each staff meeting.

Keep an office diary which contains all your appointments, and insist that all staff enter in it events in which they or their classes are involved, as well as courses and other absences known about in advance. This should avoid the persistent problem of double booking. Leave this diary where everyone can see it, and emphasise that it is not confidential. Don't take it with you when you go to meetings; keep your own diary as well. An office diary is no good if it is not always available for people to consult and update.

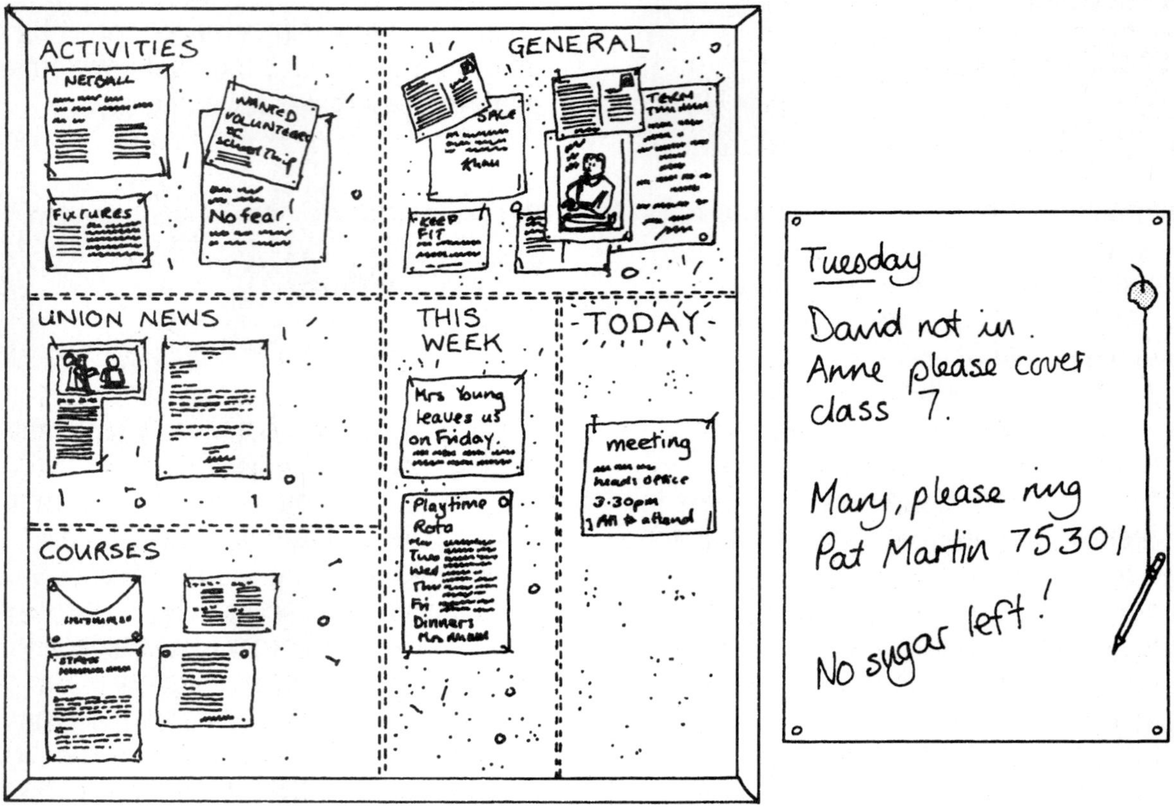

Notice boards

Keep a small, well-marked and colourful area of your staffroom notice board clear of the usual type of notice. Label it 'TODAY', and make it known that this area is only for important notices that concern the day in question. When it becomes necessary to display such a notice it should draw attention. Leave it up during that day, then make sure it is removed.

Try labelling a section of the board 'THIS WEEK'. Each Friday, pin up a list of the important dates for the following week and write in the main events from the office diary. If staff are due to be away, if activities are cancelled or re-timed, if there are important visitors or planned meetings, or if there are any important changes to the routine, write them in. Your staff will soon respect this notice as a source of information and will look at it habitually. If you use your notice board to pin up duty rotas and timetables, make sure that everyone has already had copies of them. This sort of notice should only be used as a reminder of what people are already supposed to know. Allocate a separate section of the notice board for union activities and let the representatives take charge of this.

Above all, don't allow the miscellaneous notices that proliferate in staffrooms to get mixed up with the more important messages on the board.

Try putting up a small black or white board in the staffroom for urgent messages. If someone has telephoned to say that they are sick, write up the cover arrangements here. Providing that it is usually kept clear, this kind of graffiti board can be useful. With encouragement, others will enter into the spirit of the thing and start writing their own notes.

Memos and messages

Many schools have an established communications system which involves the circulation of memos and messages between headteacher and staff.

If you are going to use this system, use it sparingly. Most teachers dislike being disturbed while working with children; it can be especially irritating if the disturbance is just for a message containing information which is irrelevant or which could have been passed on in another way.

It is best to keep message sheets or memos for urgent messages, or for pieces of information which it is vital that everyone receives. If the memo is to be circulated around the staff, ask each person to initial it to indicate that they have read it before they pass it on.

Memos are a useful way of telling everyone something which would be rathercomplex to explain individually in person. It should not be used as a way of criticising or of giving bad news. This is better done in person.

Pigeon-holes

Try to arrange for each member of staff to have somewhere where they can receive their mail and messages. In many schools the accepted procedure involves the secretary or welfare officer trailing round the classrooms delivering mail by hand, or leaving a pile of assorted items in the staffroom in the hope that the addressees will find them.

The simple and relatively cheap expedient of providing everyone with a pigeon-hole or box saves a great deal of leg-work, improves the prospects of effective communication and neatly shifts the burden on to the staff to empty their pigeon-holes regularly if they want to be kept informed. One very effective way of ensuring that pigeon-holes are emptied at least once a month is to put payslips in them. Once emptying the pigeon-holes becomes a habit, they will be useful for passing messages. Don't forget to include boxes for everyone, including part-timers and peripatetics.

A system of pigeon-holes can be a useful clearing house for the sort of publicity material which arrives in school in great abundance. You or your secretary can look at the mail and decide to pass it on to individual teachers according to their curricular or age-group interest. This at least ensures that someone who may be interested has the opportunity of seeing and responding to the material.

Passing round documents

Sometimes documents arrive in school which the headteacher feels everyone should have the opportunity to read. There are rarely enough copies for everyone, so the problem arises of how to ensure that all the staff see the document within a relatively short time.

If you are lucky enough to receive or obtain more than one copy of important documents, you can circulate each copy to a limited number of people. Used in conjunction with the pigeon-holes (providing the document is not too weighty), this should ensure a wider readership. If you have only one copy of an important document, and photocopying is out of the question, the only way to ensure that everyone sees it may be to circulate the document among the staff with a list of names to be ticked off to show that each person has read it.

Message books

Some schools find that an effective way of keeping everyone informed is to use a message book or folder. This folder, circulated daily, contains messages for staff, and any relevant reading material. This system does have a number of important drawbacks.

First of all, many teachers quite understandably dislike being disturbed in class, and this should never be underestimated. It is a little unfair to expect teachers to read and absorb a large quantity of material under such circumstances.

If you use this system, limit your messages to straightforward information, and find an alternative method for circulating the more bulky material. It is also important that the message book is kept readily available for those who want to reread information which they may not have taken in fully earlier on.

A two-way process

Communication implies a two-way process, but so far we have looked only at the passage of information from headteacher to staff.

Communication within a school is only complete when the process works both ways. To what extent do you listen and respond to the comments, requests and statements made by the staff? What opportunities are there for communication to occur? How effective is this process in the move towards greater team-work and understanding among those who work in the school?

It may be useful to ask yourself the following questions. If you have set up a network of communication which involves circulating documents to all staff, and distributing certain material selectively to teachers according to what you judge to be their interests and responsibilities, what happens then? Is the circulation approach just a useful means of disposing of vast amounts of 'junk mail' and other documents which you haven't the time or the inclination to read? Are you really inviting people to respond, or are you just getting things off your back?

You may arrive at some rather worrying conclusions. Staff will soon judge whether you are really seeking their views on incoming material, or whether they are being used as a means of disposal which your conscience finds more acceptable than the waste-paper bin.

If a school's communications network consists solely of notices and messages pinned to boards and placed in pigeon-holes, if staff meetings comprise lengthy pronouncements by the headteacher, and if members of staff feel unable or unwilling to respond positively or critically, then communication will be poor, however efficient it may appear superficially.

How can you achieve a situation in which the two-way process operates successfully?

Firstly, you as headteacher must demonstrate a willingness to listen to and, if appropriate, accept criticism and suggestions for alternative courses of action. Constructive criticism should never be viewed as a threat. Indeed, you may gain respect and strengthen your position among the staff by responding to advice and criticism in a positive way.

Consultation is part of communication, and you must be prepared to concede that the person you consult may have a better idea than you. The headteacher who regularly consults his staff without taking note of suggestions and advice, or who only seeks advice from those who share his views, will lose credibility. Faced with this sort of behaviour on the part of the head, the staff will stop responding to the consultation process, and will become cynical.

You must achieve a balance between two extremes; the paternalistic headteacher who makes all judgements and decisions for the staff, and the one who asks for everyone's comments, and receives so much conflicting advice that he doesn't know how to act.

The communication process must include a way of making the staff aware of decisions for which they have collective responsibility, as well as those for which the headteacher takes sole responsibility. The extent to which one type of decision or the other predominates is determined by the sort of regime operating in the school. There may be occasions, even in schools which are run along very democratic lines, when the headteacher has to take a decision without consulting the staff about it beforehand. The staff must be aware of the circumstances which make this sort of unilateral decision necessary.

Face to face

One characteristic of a good headteacher is the ability to listen. You have to take time to listen to the comments and requests made by individual teachers, and to be perceptive in interpreting what the message really is. Few teachers will criticise a colleague openly to the headteacher, but they may, through implication, suggest that you would do well to make yourself aware of particular difficulties which a teacher is experiencing or creating.

If you respond to this type of indirect approach, the staff will develop the confidence to use it again and will respect you for being perceptive. If you ignore the approach, the staff will feel a lack of communication and may withdraw and become isolated, or perhaps worse, develop their own ways of dealing with such problems, bypassing the headteacher.

A useful tool for communication is informal one-to-one meeting between headteacher and teacher. If you think about it, there are very few opportunities in the busy school day when a member of staff can be sure of an undisturbed session of forty minutes or an hour with the headteacher to talk about his work, professional development, relationships with colleagues or even personal problems. At least once a term, try to offer each member of staff the opportunity to meet you in an informal way in your room, to talk about any issues

which either of you wish to raise. Because the meeting is scheduled in advance, both parties have some time to think about what they are going to say. Try to sort out and agree upon some sort of agenda in advance which will serve to channel your discussion.

Staff communication

If the staff are entitled to expect effective communication from the headteacher, it is only fair that the reverse should also be true. You are entitled to know what your staff are doing in the classroom, in their other responsibilities, and in any other matter that directly affects the welfare of the school. This obligation on the part of staff even extends to letting you know about personal and health problems which may reduce their standard of performance at work.

You also have a right to expect that staff who are unable to attend because of sickness, or for any other reason, should get a message to you as soon as possible. You might like to give staff your home telephone number, to encourage them to give you the greatest possible advance notice of an absence. It is also helpful, but of course not always easy, for the teacher to indicate how long the absence is likely to be.

Contingency plans
As an extension of this principle, encourage staff to make contingency plans for those occasions when they are absent at short notice. This will be of great help to the supply teacher, and will also benefit the children in the absent teacher's class.

The following is a list of basic information which should be readily available in every classroom so that a replacement teacher can take over at short notice without too much loss of continuity. It will make a useful starting point for a staff discussion on contingency plans.

- A list of the children's names.
- A list of working groups, including seating arrangements within the class where appropriate.
- A basic and general working timetable for each day.
- Details of any out-of-class or shared activities.
- Some record of each child's progress through published or school-based schemes if appropriate.
- Details of any other staff who are timetabled to work in the class on a particular day (welfare staff, support teachers, instrumental teachers and any others).
- A short list of where to find the basic classroom requirements such as stationery and registers.

There are many things which could be added to this list, and many conscientious teachers carry out this sort of preparation as a matter of course. However, if this routine is established as common practice, it does wonders for school communication.

Being available to the staff

Another very important issue which comes under the heading of communication is that of availability and approachability. It is important to consider the ways in which a headteacher can develop and improve communications by being available to staff.

It has always been one of the acknowledged roles of the deputy head to act as an intermediary between staff and headteacher and to convey to the head the feelings and concerns of the staff. Although there may be times when an intermediary is useful, any headteacher in a primary school who routinely requires a third party to tell him what the staff are worried about is failing in one of his most important duties, that of good communication.

There are, of course, times when staff are likely to be reluctant to approach the headteacher directly, particularly over sensitive matters, but you should try to be as approachable as possible in order to keep these times to the absolute minimum.

There can be no greater compliment for a headteacher than to have one of the staff come along, unprompted, to discuss a professional or personal problem. Such an action implies trust, confidence and respect, and is to be taken as a sign of success in the area of communication.

The opposite of this situation, where everyone in the school except the headteacher knows the personal or professional difficulties a colleague is experiencing, is certainly to be avoided. The headteacher should be seen as someone who is able to balance the needs of the school against the needs of the individual, and to exercise a fair judgement.

Success in this field is only possible if the headteacher is someone the staff feel able to talk to, and to whom they have fairly free access. The headteacher's relationship with staff usually has to be worked at. Few of us, unfortunately, are liked and respected by all we meet; the only solution is hard work.

Don't overlook small details. The following considerations may seem minor, but they are nevertheless important.

- How do you address people?
- Are you happy on first name terms?
- Do you show interest in what staff are doing?
- Are you always thought of as critical, or are you sometimes positive and constructive?

Good communication is a two-way process, but it is ultimately the responsibility of the headteacher to ensure that an efficient and effective system of communication operates in his school.

Chapter Five

Meetings in school

One headteacher for whom I worked liked to run meetings at which everyone had the chance to make a contribution on every item. She hoped this would help us to move towards a unity of conclusion. Everyone made a contribution, but most of us were at odds with each other, and unity was the last thing we moved towards. The head would then conclude by saying, 'Well, this is how I would do it,' and then suggest an approach to adopt. There would usually be a reluctant nodding agreement to this and we would move on to the next business. When I asked her why she always took this course of action, she said, 'If they agree to my suggestion, at least one of us will be happy, and I can see no reason why that one person shouldn't be me.'

In another school the routine meetings were held about twice a term. The staff would gather at lunchtime in the staffroom and occupy the various chairs, both easy and upright, which filled the room. As no one bothered to rearrange the room, it meant that some of those present were facing in opposite directions.

Most of the staff brought something to eat with them, ranging from school lunches to packets of sandwiches and bags of chips from the local shop. One teacher always spent her break-times knitting, so the proceedings were accompanied by the clack of needles.

These meetings were notable for the length of the monologues given by the headteacher and for the profundity of the silence from the staff. This silence was taken by the head as a symbol of the respect with which his ideas were held by the staff, and of their complete agreement.

When the odd interruption did occur from one of the teachers, the head would raise his voice. Unfortunately, once the intervention had been successfully dealt with, he would usually continue at the same pitch, with the result that by the end of the meeting he would be almost shouting at us.

When the meeting ended, usually about two minutes before the start of afternoon school, the head would leave the staffroom. Then a hubbub of noise would erupt from the teachers. Complaints would be made about the lack of consultation and communication, and a whole litany of the head's shortcomings and failures would be recited. Plans would be made and contingency arrangements discussed to deal with this latest imposition on teacher time and professional freedom. More team spirit was engendered and more decisions were taken in those two hectic minutes than in the whole of the previous hour. In this way the school was kept going, and some sort of organisation and communication system was generated — despite, rather than because of the formal staff meetings.

These two examples, by no means unusual or extreme in the folklore of education, illustrate a few of the problems which a headteacher must consider when thinking about the form which staff meetings should take.

Meetings in primary schools can take many different forms. Some of the more common forms may not even be recognised by the participants as meetings, but they can still be extremely productive amd worthwhile.

It is easy to forget that a planning meeting, a curriculum discussion or a conference on the progress of a particular child does not have to take place in a boardroom atmosphere in order to be valuable. An animated discussion in the corner of the staffroom over a cup of coffee often produces results which it would be difficult to obtain in any other situation.

Ingredients for success

There are a number of key ingredients for a successful meeting, whether it is taking place in a primary school or in an international corporation. The absence of one or more of them may result in wasted time, frustration and inefficiency.

Purpose

It might seem obvious that a meeting must have a purpose, but most of us have sat through meetings which have lacked precisely this. We are all familiar with the type of comments made afterwards — 'What was that all about?' and 'What a waste of time!'

Those attending the meeting should know what they are there to discuss, and what their terms of reference are. If there is no clear agenda, there should be no meeting; if the matters being discussed are outside the powers of those attending to decide, there is little point in coming together to talk about them.

Meetings should have aims. It should be clear what must be discussed, resolved or decided by the end of the meeting. The absence of a sense of purpose leads to side-tracking, red herrings and a singular lack of commitment from those attending.

Time limit
Ideally, a meeting should work to a deadline. Out of courtesy to those attending, as well as in the cause of greater efficiency, there should be a fairly accurate statement before a meeting begins of how long will be spent on each item and at what time the meeting will end. There should be no such thing as an open-ended meeting; a specified time limit gives contributors the incentive to stick to the point. Prompt starts and finishes should be the rule.

Further action
Finally, a meeting should be a pointer to further action. This may be action by groups or individuals, or even just a decision to have a further meeting. Any meeting which ends without some form of resolution to take further action has been wasted.

How often?

Regular, organised staff meetings are, in many primary schools, a comparative innovation. Before the arrival of directed time, staff meetings tended to be occasional events — perhaps only termly or even annually. Their main use was in arranging the dates of school events, announcing decisions about aspects of organisation, and allowing staff the opportunity to discuss minor administrative or curricular issues. As everyone was attending on a 'voluntary' basis, the timing and frequency of the meetings were often arranged carefully so as not to stretch goodwill too far. Where the meetings were widely spaced, it was difficult for anyone to remember what was agreed at the last one, and there was little chance of progression or continuity between meetings.

Directed time changed all this. Some headteachers felt that they should be able to account for their staff for every one of the 1,265 hours of directed time per year. This meant that regular weekly or even twice-weekly staff meetings were established in some schools, whether they were needed or not. In certain schools the staff meeting changed rapidly from a cosy, traditional event relying mainly on goodwill and good memory, to a pressing obligation which required stamina, commitment and a thorough knowledge of current issues and the rules of debate.

This is, of course, a comparison of extremes. Many schools managed the change without too many problems, and it is worth considering the reasons for their success.

You have a difficult choice to make when considering how often to call meetings. Do you set up a regular staff meeting, with the likelihood that there will be too much or too little business at any one meeting, or do you establish a custom of calling the staff together as required?

The first option has clear advantages in terms of planning and convenience. If staff know that they have a regular commitment on a certain day of the week or month throughout the year, they can plan around this. On the other hand, there may be difficulties if pressure of business requires additional, unplanned meetings. An extra meeting called within the context of directed time may impose pressures on the system, especially if it is arranged at short notice.

The second option, which involves agreeing to call staff meetings as required, means that the frequency of meetings reflects the level of business, but it has the disadvantage of being difficult to plan for and also of resulting in an uneven flow of activity throughout the year.

You will have to make your own decisions about the regularity and structure of staff meetings. You will also have to demonstrate to staff that such meetings are both necessary and effective.

What has gone before will have an effect on the staff's response to change. If meetings have previously been an annual affair, staff may show initial reluctance, and even resentment, at being called upon for a greater commitment in the form of a monthly meeting. If, on the other hand, meetings have previously been held weekly and you are proposing fortnightly or monthly gatherings instead, you will probably get a much more positive reaction to the change.

It is important not to take too much notice of the relative popularity or unpopularity of change. Staff in a school where there have been too few meetings may demonstrate their discontent outwardly, while realising the importance of more frequent consultation and its beneficial effect both on their own professional development and on the development of the school as a whole. Remember, though, that meetings must be seen to be purposeful, and that they must always be moving towards some conclusion.

Who attends?

The headteacher has to decide who should attend meetings. Does everyone need to attend each meeting? Do non-teaching staff always need to be there?

As usual, it is a question of balance. Some people will be offended if they are not included in meetings, whereas others will resent having to attend meetings which they don't think directly concern them.

Most people like to feel involved, even if they don't feel able to make contributions. It is often possible to reach a satisfactory compromise, in the case of non-teaching staff such as nursery nurses or welfare assistants, by impressing on individuals whose attendance is not vital that, while they are welcome to attend, they are not obliged to do so.

Working parties

Smaller groups such as working parties or sub-committees can be set up, comprising either staff members with expertise in the relevant area or others who have expressed willingness to be involved. These smaller groups will be able to meet separately from the main staff meetings, and then report back to the full group.

There are two clear advantages to this system. Small groups tend to work far more efficiently than large groups; also they are made up of people who have expertise and active interest in the subject, and who are willing to give time to the project in hand. The small group in this case does the majority of the work, but the large group is kept well informed and is therefore able to make the significant decisions.

There will be a Staff Meeting on Wednesday June 6 at 3.45pm in Room 16.

AGENDA

1. Matters arising from previous meeting.
2. To consider the draft special needs policy (copy attached). Special needs co-ordinator to report.
3. Alterations to dates and arrangements for the term.
4. Reports from working parties:
   i) Record-keeping group;
   ii) National Curriculum group;
   iii) Home/school liaison group.
5. Any other business. Please give advance notice to allow for time to be made available.
6. Date of next meeting.

Preparation

Whether the staff meeting involves the whole staff or just a few people, the preparation for the meeting will be much the same.

Agendas

There should be some form of agenda — either written and circulated beforehand, or a verbal indication to each person attending of the subjects which it is proposed to discuss. The reason for this is obvious: those taking part cannot be expected to be prepared to take part in discussions if they do not know in advance what the subject of the meeting is to be. The surprise element should have no place in staff meetings.

Circulating information

You may need to circulate documents before the meeting. It is bad practice to issue sheaves of papers during a meeting and expect everyone to read them on the spot, consider their contents and then instantly engage in purposeful discussion about them.

Reading documents at meetings is a waste of time. Some people read faster than others and will therefore be frustrated by the delay while they wait for the rest to catch up. The slower readers may pretend to have finished in order not to appear slow, or to avoid holding up the meeting.

The chances are that few of the participants will absorb the information. It is far better to give out any necessary information well in advance and let people read it in their own time.

The meeting room

Meetings can be businesslike without being officious and a brisk, efficient atmosphere, aided by properly prepared agenda and papers, should help to stimulate the desired response. Giving some thought to the layout and furniture of the meeting room also helps to create the right atmosphere.

Think about the room to be used — always assuming you have a choice. Everyone needs somewhere to sit, so make sure you have enough chairs. There will usually be latecomers. This is irritating enough, but it can be made even more frustrating for all concerned if they then have to depart to distant parts of the school in search of chairs. Everyone should have somewhere to rest their papers. Are you able to provide tables?

The staffroom is seldom ideal for a meeting. It may be equipped with easy chairs which, although comfortable, are not the best form of seating for a meeting; firm, high-backed chairs are better. If you have a table large enough, arrange chairs around it to allow everyone to face their colleagues and to have somewhere to put their papers. Decide where you are going to sit. Don't always make this at the head of the table, and don't sit next to the same people every time.

Conducting the meeting

Once everyone is assembled, properly prepared with agenda and papers, you can get down to business.

Starting on time

Try, above all, to begin the meeting promptly. This is important both out of consideration to those who have arrived on time and as a reminder to those who are late. If people think that meetings never begin on time, they will make less effort to be punctual, with the result that the start will get later and later. Prompt starts and finishes should be a priority.

Important ingredients

The essential ingredients of most meetings are communication, discussion, debate and agreement.

The last three ingredients are perhaps the most important. You don't really need a meeting to tell people things, but you do need one if you want their views and opinions, and if you want to reach a decision. If you want a decision, you have to accept that it might not be entirely in line with your own thoughts on the subject.

Matters in hand

The matters which you want to discuss at the meeting should have been listed on the agenda. If the meeting is concerned purely with administration – setting dates for future staff meetings, for example – it is enough for you to outline what you are proposing and ask if there are any problems with this.

On matters of policy, you should arrange to present an outline for discussion, preferably in the form of a document circulated well before the meeting.

If, for example, you wish to discuss a possible policy for 'education for personal relationships' within the school, you might have asked teachers in a working party to draft an outline of proposals and circulate this before the meeting. At the meeting, ask people to comment on the outline or raise any points they wish to be considered. Take notes throughout the discussion, and at the end of an agreed time limit, sum up and move on to the next item. Your summing up might be along the lines of 'There seems to be general agreement about ...'. There should be no need to take votes; your discussion should move to a consensus of opinion.

If you are genuinely trying to foster a co-operative, team approach to decision-making and policy matters in the school, it is not helpful for you to make your position clear too early on in the discussion. Nor will it help team-building if you side too readily with one or more people, without seeming to consider all aspects and points of view. In this case, the staff will decide that if minds are already made up, there is little point in discussion. They will then look upon staff meetings as a charade.

Questions of formality

There are some schools where staff meetings successfully take the form of an open forum and where everyone contributes on an informal basis. However, unless you feel confident with this approach, it is far better to organise meetings along more formal lines, with a chairperson. Full staff meetings are usually chaired by the headteacher, but this doesn't always have to be the case. The deputy needs experience in this role and may prove to be better at it, while other senior members of staff might be the best people to chair discussions on matters relating to their specific responsibilities.

Conducting a meeting is an art. Most of us have sat through good meetings and bad meetings. The difference between them is often the attitude of the chairperson. The role of chairperson can be a difficult one and is not always compatible with the traditional role of the headteacher. Chairpersons often need to be neutral; they may occasionally need to adopt a passive attitude, and they sometimes need to be reticent.

Handling the different characters present at meetings requires a subtle combination of experience, tact and skill. What you want as headteacher is a rapid tactic for using the strengths and minimising the weaknesses of your staff, while ensuring a flow of business and a satisfactory conclusion to the meeting.

Strategies for managing meetings

Coping with silence

Preparation, setting time limits and agreeing an agenda will all help to make a meeting more successful, but some things are more difficult to handle. How do you cope with silence? Do you take a lack of reaction to mean approval, disapproval, incomprehension or a total lack of interest?

One simple explanation for silence – and one which is often overlooked by heads – is tiredness. If the meeting is straight after school, teachers are trying to unwind from the demands of the classroom. Engaging in lively and intellectually demanding debate may be the furthest thing from their minds.

There may be no alternative to the after-school meeting; lunchtimes are often worse. Some schools have experimented successfully with meeting early in the morning, and it might be worth considering this. But if you have to meet at the end of the afternoon, set the meeting for fifteen or twenty minutes after the end of school to give everyone time to sort themselves out and perhaps take some refreshment.

Another explanation for silence is the headteacher's dominance of the meeting. However enlightened and democratic you may be, you are still 'the boss' and teachers may be reluctant to voice their thoughts, particularly if they appear to contradict your views.

If you are embarrassed by silence, the chances are that others in the room are equally embarrassed. Try a game of bluff. If no one says anything, resist the temptation to fill the vacuum. Keep quiet and see who breaks the silence first. You may find that several people begin talking at once, and that you then have a problem of order to deal with, but at least the impasse will have been broken.

Keeping to the point

Another obstruction to the smooth running of staff meetings is the person who insists on talking off the point. This requires firm but sensitive handling and a keen awareness of what is relevant to the point under discussion.

The skill lies in judging the value of an individual's contribution. You have to avoid cutting people off short and making them feel silly, while at the same time ensuring that comments are largely relevant.

Involving everyone

If you are chairperson, you also need to make sure that everyone present is involved in the meeting. This can be difficult if you have staff members who habitually say little. Try to draw them into the discussion, particularly where you know they have expertise or interest, but be careful of turning the spotlight on them so that the whole gathering is sitting expectantly waiting for their views. They may never forgive you, with the result that they never contribute again.

The chairperson has to control the stronger members of the group, who may nevertheless have useful points to put, while encouraging the quieter, more reticent members. In this situation, moving towards a consensus is often difficult.

Testing the water

You may find it advantageous to canvass opinion before the meeting in order to get some idea of likely support or opposition for your proposals. This is also a chance to try a bit of subtle persuasion. In this way you will have a clearer idea of the way the meeting is likely to go. The meeting will then be less protracted, and you will avoid appearing to be a minority voice fighting against opposition.

Stating the options

One useful technique is to have in your mind, before the meeting begins, a list of options which you would find acceptable, given your professional experience and knowledge of what is practical. At some stage in the meeting you can present these to the group. The most satisfactory outcome may be to agree on one of these options; this will avoid the pitfall of seeming to impose a single idea on the staff. This method is a useful compromise, falling short of the full democratic process which can prove difficult to handle or to live with if the staff decision is in favour of a policy you find unacceptable.

Recording the proceedings

Opinions vary about the wisdom of taking minutes at staff meetings. Some people find the presence of a minute-taking secretary inhibiting. Others feel that a staff meeting is essentially an informal gathering, and they dislike any course of action which appears to make it too formal.

There are great advantages to having minutes for a meeting, although it is sensible to limit the minutes to brief notes of the decisions taken and any objections raised. It is certainly useful to detail any courses of action resulting from the meeting and to name the people who will be responsible for these. This serves to remind the people concerned what they should be doing before the next meeting, and helps to ensure that things happen reasonably quickly. A review of what was decided at the last meeting also provides a very good starting point for the next meeting.

A useful idea is to have a rota for note-taking. Apart from sharing the load, this tends to even out bias and prejudices in the minutes. It is best to make the minutes available to everyone as soon as possible after the meeting.

Remember, too, that notes of a meeting serve to inform those who were not present about what was discussed. Pin up some notes on a board the next day, and get everyone to initial the notes to confirm that they have read and agree with them. Keep the completed sheet for further reference in case of difficulties or queries later on, and to satisfy yourself that everyone has seen it.

Continuity of purpose

It is possible to find schools where staff meetings occur as isolated events, without continuity. This is a strange phenomenon, but one which has been widespread. Matters are discussed by the whole staff, and decisions are arrived at, but everyone goes away, returns to their classroom and carries on exactly as before. When the next meeting occurs, perhaps a month later, no mention is made of previous discussions, new matters are considered and the same cycle repeats itself.

By and large teachers don't like attending meetings. They see them as obstacles to what is undeniably their real work in the classroom. They can't be blamed for this attitude; after all, they are trained professionals who have an important and valuable job to do. Unless meetings are purposeful and make a positive contribution to the job of teaching, teachers cannot be expected to welcome them.

One way in which you can help is to introduce an element of continuity into the meetings. Minutes have already been discussed as a way of reminding people about what has gone before, but it also helps to include on the agenda a regular review of certain items, so that teachers are informed of developments and will begin to see how things are progressing. This policy helps when you are trying to develop a whole-school approach to matters like the curriculum and professional development, and it can help remove the feelings of isolation which most teachers experience occasionally.

The success of a school depends in no short measure upon the amount of communication, consultation and collective decision-making which takes place in the course of day-to-day activities. The possibility of successful and effective 'management by edict' has long disappeared. The need for members of staff to talk to each other, share their views and problems and arrive at a common purpose has never been greater.

Chapter Six

Towards a management structure

There is no single correct way of managing a school. If you look at a dozen different schools, you will find a dozen different ways of organising staff and resources, each developed to suit particular circumstances and areas of expertise. Before you can begin to devise your own management structure, you need to think about what your aims are and how you might achieve them.

The purpose of this chapter is to examine some of the possible ways of organising schools to allow for delegation in a number of areas and to create some form of management structure.

Any examination of this sort should take account of the wide range of difficulties which individual schools face, the variation in teachers' skills, talents and abilities and, perhaps most important of all, the differences which arise in terms of staffing and resources.

For these reasons it is impossible to produce a management formula for a 'typical' school. There is no such thing as a typical primary school.

The traditions of primary school management

Let's start by considering some of the factors which can influence one's view of primary school management structures in general.

Who is the expert?
There is an assumption, which must be challenged openly and rapidly, that the headteacher always knows best; that he or she knows more about the curriculum, is a better teacher, and can plan and manage better than anyone else in the school.

Until very recently, most primary school headteachers were appointed on the basis of a successful career in the classroom and some management experience as a deputy head. Some local authorities had training programmes for deputies, and some had induction programmes for new headteachers, but it was left largely to the individual to seek relevant courses and guidance.

Going into a new school in a new role puts the headteacher into the position of a learner. There are benefits to be gained from accepting this, and from drawing on the experience of colleagues both in and out of the school. This approach is perfectly compatible with the role of the headteacher as the leader of a team of professionals; the leader of a group should not be expected to possess all the skills of the group members, or to be able to do their jobs better than they can.

If you are able to accept this view and recognise the difference between being a team leader and a master craftsman, then you can go on to try a different approach to school management.

The appeal of administration
The second factor is that not every teacher wants to become involved in school administration. Most people go into teaching because of their wish to be with children and to be involved in the active side of education, rather than because they see teaching as a career offering opportunities to consult and influence colleagues, to lead teams of professionals, and to be involved in the induction and training of other teachers. This applies equally to teachers who subsequently become headteachers and deputies.

Who needs it?
Opinions vary about the desirability of a management structure in a primary school. Some would argue that schools have managed for many years with the headteacher and secretary organising everything, and that teachers should be left to get on with their job. This is very much a minority viewpoint nowadays, and the need for some delegation is widely recognised. The old scale posts, and now incentive allowances, have made such delegation possible.

Headteachers have had to overcome numerous difficulties in coming to terms with the scale post structure. These difficulties have included matching the posts available to the skills and interests of the staff and to the tasks needing to be tackled, and having to motivate those members of staff without scale posts or 'allowances'.

The problem arises in part from the fact that primary schools, unlike secondary schools, have no traditional hierarchical structure. Secondary schools are used to the idea of department heads, year group heads, senior teachers and directors of studies. In primaries there is seldom a post between teacher and deputy, and where posts such as 'head of lower school' have been created, they have sometimes been viewed as anomalies.

The incentive allowance idea was supposed to give governors and headteachers the chance to rationalise management structures and to reward 'good classroom teachers'. However, it was not clear whether the incentive was intended to make teachers do a better job, to motivate them to maintain standards, to encourage them to stay at the school, to attract others to seek posts at the school, or to force those who did not receive the incentive to look elsewhere. Incentives were spread rather thinly, and many schools found themselves with perhaps only one 'A' post to offer.

Management arrangements

You may find the following suggestions helpful, especially with pressures on primary schools at their current high level. However, the suggestions take into account a number of assumptions with which all headteachers may not agree.

The use of incentive allowances
If you accept that all primary schools, regardless of size, have the same areas of the curriculum to cover, it seems absurd to use incentive allowances to reward teachers who manage particular aspects of the curriculum while denying such rewards to colleagues who manage equally important areas. Why, for instance, should the single 'A' post in a small school go to the language co-ordinator, while the other curriculum leaders remain on Main Professional Grade?

Such a policy is divisive and implies value judgements about the relative worth of different curricular areas. It also overlooks the fact that an 'A' allowance can be used in different ways, either for specific projects over limited periods or as a reward for good class-teaching.

To embark on a policy of awarding allowances for specific curriculum areas entails the risk of finding yourself back in the old scale post situation, with limited opportunity for variation and a fair share of curricular dinosaurs and white elephants.

The wide variation in size between primary schools — from a couple of dozen children to over 500 — presents different levels and types of challenge to headteachers. This is not always recognised in the allocation of allowances. If, for example, it is acknowledged that every school needs to provide music for its pupils, why is it acceptable for this to be provided in a small school by a Main Professional Grade teacher, while a large school may have the chance of attracting a specialist teacher with an 'A' or 'B' allowance? There can be little justification for using posts for curriculum organisation.

Delegating management
Schools of different sizes will have different management requirements. The headteacher of any school has overall management responsibilities, but these increase with the size of the school. It is in

this context that the best use of incentive posts can be made. In addition to day-to-day organisational and administrative duties, there are a number of specific management roles which the headteacher has to adopt, and which can usefully and effectively be delegated to others, thus forming a management team. The following are some of the management roles which could be delegated.

- Staff management. This involves timetabling, rotas and arranging cover for absences.
- INSET. The staff member responsible for INSET will organise course information, allocate funds, plan school INSET days, and balance the needs of the school with those of the individual. She will lead the staff in the preparation of a development plan.
- Special needs. A responsibility for special needs involves maintaining an overview of special needs provision in the school and ensuring the suitable application of criteria. Liaison with outside agencies and reviews of the use of in-school support will also be important.
- Record-keeping and assessment. This involves reviewing and assessing school record-keeping policy, and monitoring assessment procedures in the light of Education Reform Act requirements.
- Induction. It will be somebody's task to ensure the smooth induction of new staff, especially probationers, and to liaise with advisory staff and teacher tutors.
- Curriculum co-ordination. This involves maintaining an overview of curricular activities – especially in the context of the National Curriculum – and liaising with subject area co-ordinators.
- Liaison. The member of staff responsible for liaison will have to make contact with new children and their families before the children start school, and liaise with local feeder establishments such as playgroups, nurseries and infant schools. It will also be important to keep up contact with secondary or infant/junior schools, to ensure a smooth transition for the children between stages. In larger schools it may be necessary to ensure continuity between the lower and upper school.
- Local Management of Schools. Someone will need to oversee the

administrative procedures connected with LMS, co-ordinating the activities of governors' sub-committees, and liaising with Local Authority officers.

• Appraisal. Someone should be responsible for the routine process of appraisal of teaching staff as determined by legal requirements.

Each of these activities has to take place, to a greater or lesser extent, in every school. The only alternative to delegation is for the head-teacher to do everything, with all that implies in terms of workload and effectiveness. I would not suggest that all of these areas should be delegated, but it is clearly desirable to share the burden if possible.

The deputy must accept a significant share of this responsibility, and those teachers who have incentive allowances should also be given a proportional share of management responsibility.

This view may not be in line with the original intention of the incentive allowance idea, but headteachers' management responsibilities have risen so much recently that it is now unrealistic to expect them to run schools single-handedly without the support and active co-operation of a management team.

The degree and type of delegation has, of course, to take account of the skills, interests and enthusiasms of the individuals concerned. It is in the best interests of the school and the individual teachers if the areas of responsibility are reviewed periodically and varied to allow for a broadening of experience. The headteacher has a responsibility to help staff to train for promotion, and to offer them the chance to prepare for future opportunities. If the jobs available are rotated on a one- or two-year cycle, new perspectives and challenges can be introduced regularly.

Collective curriculum responsibility

If all the posts are allocated to distinct management roles, who will look after the curriculum? Primary teachers have always accepted implicitly a role in curriculum management. Even in the days of scale posts for maths, language and other curriculum areas, to a large extent class-teachers still taught right across the curriculum and managed their own class's learning in each area. It is a short, though sometimes hazardous step from this situation to one in which teachers have a collective involvement in curriculum planning for the whole school, under the direction of one teacher with a particular expertise or interest.

It is important to be very careful to maintain fairness here. If everyone is involved in the process of curriculum planning, it will be easier to implement. If every teacher adopts a curriculum leadership role in a specific area, individual teachers will be less likely to resent what they are being asked to do.

In reality you are likely to find that such resentment is rare. Most teachers are willing to accept a degree of additional responsibility, provided the headteacher's expectations are made clear, and as long as individual limitations are recognised and acknowledged.

The feeling that everyone is in the same position helps to smooth the transition to this style of collective responsibility. It can help individual teachers to know that everyone is experiencing similar difficulties and having to overcome similar problems. It is important that teachers who have incentive allowances for managerial responsibilities also have the same curricular responsibilities as their colleagues.

The curriculum co-ordinator's role
What is likely to be expected of the teachers once they have each adopted a curriculum leadership role? How does this role fit into the idea of corporate decision-making?

Under the scale post system, the post-holder in a particular subject had certain key duties: policy-making, providing resources and consultancy (in other words, drawing up and reviewing work programmes, ordering stock and answering queries from staff).

These three duties did not necessarily require the post-holder to involve colleagues in decision making, nor did they imply a leadership role. An acceptable modern interpretation of the role of curriculum co-ordinator would still include the consultancy aspect, because there needs to be someone in the school who, even if he doesn't have all the answers, knows where to find them. The consultancy role also includes a requirement to work alongside colleagues in an advisory capacity if necessary, in order to assist them with particular difficulties. The teachers involved must therefore build the trust, confidence and respect of colleagues, and be approachable and available. As headteacher, you need to monitor this process carefully.

Resources
Ordering resources is still a part of the role of the curriculum co-ordinator, but this has been subtly changed by the obligation to confer. Providing staff with books and materials is one thing; providing them with the resources they want and in which they have confidence is quite another. The co-ordinator's job is to appraise the available material, present a range of possible options to staff, respond to staff requests and criticism and then balance this against the need to provide breadth and balance within the curriculum. It is probable that this will have to be done within a budgetary constraint, since the headteacher may also have delegated the financial responsibility.

If the corporate decision-making process is to be adopted seriously, the role of the co-ordinator in respect of policy statements will change from that of provider to that of enabler. As all staff will be involved in the policy- and syllabus-building, the co-ordinator must take the role of leader in the discussion.

Training for leadership

The teachers will vary greatly in their expertise and ability as leaders. There are important implications for staff training, which you need to address at an early stage. Teachers themselves will benefit from training, and so will the development of the school, so there must be no short cuts. Simply giving someone a responsibility and a title — even if you pay them for it — doesn't make them able to do the job. Support, training and time are all essential.

Passing on INSET information

You may have appointed a member of staff as INSET co-ordinator for the school. Their job would be to find out about relevant courses, or at least to know who to contact to find out about them, and then to pass on the information to the curriculum co-ordinators concerned. As a general rule, INSET co-ordinators should try the following sources of information:

- The LEA. They will know about courses at teachers' centres, run by the advisory service.
- The local adviser for the relevant subject area. He may know about courses outside your area, perhaps run in conjunction with another LEA.
- University institutes of education or other outside sources such as industrial societies.

Long-term plans

The establishment of a curriculum management structure, like any other major change, takes time. Staff recruitment may be affected by the need to appoint teachers with particular levels of expertise and interest.

As with management responsibilities, there are advantages in rotating teachers' curriculum responsibilities from time to time in order to broaden experience and to introduce new perspectives. The fact that the teachers will not be tied to specific responsibilities by contracts and detailed job descriptions makes this task easier than it was previously.

A senior management team

If you have allocated curriculum responsibilities to all your teachers, so that at least most of the accepted subject areas have someone co-ordinating activities, and if you also have teachers on incentive allowances covering some of the recognised management areas, is there a case for creating and building a senior management team?

Many organisations, including schools, have benefited from the use of a management team. In a school such a team would comprise senior teaching staff, working with the headteacher to formulate policy and exercise a management function. The formation of such a group follows naturally from the policy of involving teachers more widely in decision-making, but it is still an important and perhaps difficult step for a headteacher to take.

You must have a high degree of confidence in the ability, skills and integrity of the members of such a group and, at the same time, you must be confident about your own position in the school. Any power-sharing exercise carries the risk of a take-over. It is essential that limits are clearly drawn; you must define what is or is not eligible for inclusion in the decision-making process by this group, and all terms of reference must be determined at the outset.

The concepts of loyalty and team-work are important in a management group. Loyalty implies a duty to be bound by group decisions, even if they go against the individual's view, and a willingness to support colleagues within the group against opposition from outside. However, care has to be taken to avoid letting the group become a clique; decisions and actions have to be justifiable, and the proceedings should be as open as the normal conventions of confidentiality permit.

Aspects of team-work

Team-work is an easier concept to describe than it is to develop. The concept of a team covers many things: leadership; a common goal; complementary skills; a shared set of rules or motives; fitness for membership. Leadership must come from the headteacher, and the success of the group depends on his or her ability in this respect.

The aims and motives of the group have to be agreed mutually, according to the circumstances of the school. They cannot realistically be determined or imposed from above. What each member can offer may be revealed quite slowly. Strengths and abilities may come to light in the course of time, and are often fully realised only when there is an opportunity to use them.

Selecting team members

In an ideal world, with unlimited staff mobility, a multitude of applicants and infinite time to select staff, it might be possible to choose the members of a management team according to what they have to offer and how this complements what is already there. In reality, the situation is very different. Headteachers who are fortunate enough to be able to appoint senior staff may be faced with a very small number of applicants. They will also be taking other factors into account, such as subject interest and age-group experience. Attempting to judge how the candidates would fit in with the other members of a team may have to take second place to more immediate demands and requirements.

The deputy head

Where does the deputy head fit into this structure, and what can be said about his role? In most primary schools the deputy has a considerable teaching commitment, and in many schools the deputies are full-time class teachers. This unfortunate fact may limit their involvement in the day-to-day running of the school. The deputy often has to take on the areas of responsibility for which no one else is available or which no one else wants. This does nothing for the self-esteem of the deputy, and does not contribute to the establishment of a clear management structure.

A working partnership

Everything that has been said about the constitution of a management team — the need to have clear areas of responsibility, the need to use individuals' strengths and allow for their weaknesses in a complementary way, and the need for mutual support — applies equally to the working partnership between the headteacher and his or her deputy.

In most primary schools, particularly the smaller ones, the deputy may have a curricular responsibility in addition to be being a class teacher. This may introduce pressures and tensions into the management role. You have to bear this in mind, and to make allowances for the difficulties and conflicts which may arise.

Above all, you must remember that a significant part of the deputy's management work, at least in the early days, is connected with training for headship. If the only management responsibility a deputy undertakes is to order the stationery or pin up the playground duty roster, then he will be ill-prepared for headship and may forfeit the chance of promotion through a lack of all-round experience.

On the other hand, if the deputy feels that he is having to do everything in the school as well as teach full time, resentment and a subsequent breakdown in your relationship with him is a real possibility. You must retain a balance between the need to present the deputy with opportunities and experiences and the temptation to over-delegate.

The role of deputy varies greatly from place to place and according to the personalities involved. It is a fairly recent development for deputies to be involved in management training, and for them to be offered opportunities to meet as a group to share common interests and concerns.

It is unfortunate that there is so little opportunity for heads and deputies to share experiences such as courses and conferences, and thus to build on the team idea. This is common practice in commerce and industry and also in education in countries such as the USA, where principals and vice-principals have a clearly defined division of responsibilities and where they seldom attend meetings and courses separately.

The art of delegation

All the approaches to school organisation and management described in this chapter require delegation. Delegation is an art, and there can be no successful management without it. The delegator must have confidence and trust in those to whom he delegates. He must recognise that other people may be able to do a job better or more quickly than he can, and he must realise that just because he is responsible or accountable for something, it does not necessarily mean that he has to do it himself. At the same time, the delegator has to accept that there may be occasions when he feels he could undertake the delegated task better and more quickly than the person to whom it has been given. There are many reasons for tolerating this situation: the need to gain experience; the need to build up confidence, or simply the need to spread the workload.

A cardinal rule of delegation is that once you have made a decision to delegate, you must limit your interference very strictly. One of the skills of delegating lies in judging the capabilities and limitations of the people to whom you are allotting tasks. Once you have been given a job to get on with, there is little worse than having the boss looking over your shoulder, offering criticism and advice and implying that he could do the job better in half the time.

Appraisal

As mentioned in Chapter 5, regular informal meetings between the headteacher and individual members of staff can be a useful means of communication. Use these meetings to discuss the individual's work and professional development, and to air any worries on either side. Interaction like this is an important prerequisite for successful formal appraisal, and in fact it can often be more beneficial than formal appraisal.

In some circumstances, appraisal by one's colleagues is as useful as appraisal by superiors. Some form of peer group appraisal might prove a useful addition to the more traditional approach. You must ensure that the result is valid and constructive, and ensure that those people who do not fit into the group still have the chance of a fair appraisal.

Chapter Seven

Planning the curriculum

It has always been assumed that teachers in primary schools know instinctively what they should be teaching. Many teachers who started their careers twenty or thirty years ago can tell stories of being left to their own devices in their probationary year, with little or no curricular guidance. They carried out their job in profound isolation, with no chance to discuss their work with colleagues. There was little or no opportunity to receive help or guidance or to influence events, and probationers felt that everyone was watching and waiting for them to make a mistake.

When problems occurred, the headteacher and staff often blamed the colleges for not training students properly. It was not until much more recently that the idea began to develop that the curriculum is an evolving thing, that the whole staff has a responsibility for its development and that the induction of new teachers into this process is a commitment which schools must accept.

The curriculum and the law

It is interesting that the 1944 Education Act, which created the foundations of the modern education system, makes little specific reference to the curriculum and certainly makes no attempt to define its content or the methods by which it is delivered. For forty years there was a trust placed — some would say naively — in heads and teachers to deliver a commonly accepted curriculum. The opportunities for anyone outside the system to criticise or influence what went on were limited.

The legislation of the 1980s destroyed the notion that it was possible to pass on the primary curriculum by a sort of folklore, and laid down basic guidelines about what should be taught.

At more or less the same time, many teachers began to develop the view that the school staff should be involved in curriculum planning and development, and that there should be regular reviews of what was going on. This is in marked contrast to the experience which many of us have had of going into a school as a new member of staff and being handed a bundle of papers which comprised 'the schemes'.

In many cases it was never really clear how these 'schemes' had originated; the headteacher may have inherited them from a predecessor or compiled them from experience, or they may have been put together from a variety of sources. Whatever the origin of the schemes, three things were nearly always true. Firstly, the staff were rarely involved in the compilation of the schemes. Secondly, they were seldom reviewed or updated. Finally, there was little evidence that any of the teachers made much use of them.

Such documents, undoubtedly a widespread feature of primary education in the fairly recent past, were held in high regard by some people. They were passed on with an element of reverence and kept in a safe place. They were above question and dispute. Teachers who disagreed with the content were required to practise a form of deceit about what went on in their classrooms.

By and large, the situation is vastly different now. A headteacher going into a school may still discover a series of box-files labelled 'Guidelines' or 'Schemes of work', but will now be expected to give them only a cursory glance before consigning them to the waste-paper basket.

Curriculum problems

Today's headteacher faces a number of new problems relating to curriculum content and policy, which must be overcome successfully at an early stage.

The first problem arises from the fact that each successive piece of legislation has made further inroads into the area of curriculum content. Local authorities must now have a written policy on the curriculum. Governors are required to have made a response to this, and have been given substantial control over curriculum content. The Government itself has defined a National Curriculum which must be delivered in every maintained school.

The headteacher and staff have a clear duty to reconcile these different views of the curriculum, to take account of their school's unique circumstances, and to produce, in consultation with the governors, a workable system which achieves the required results while retaining professional integrity.

The art of curriculum management lies in matching what should be going on with what is practical in the classroom. For example, the governors may have been advised that the school should have a policy on 'education for personal relationships'. They put this to the staff, and the staff then spend a considerable time producing a programme which both governors and parents agree is suitable. However, the staff have to implement the programme in the classroom, and so there will be constant fine adjustments to allow for individual problems.

Achieving staff involvement

Curriculum planning is no longer the sole responsibility of the headteacher, and in order to ensure effective curriculum implementation and delivery, the whole staff must be involved at every stage of development.

How is this achieved? What options are available to the headteacher?

The following examples show different approaches to the construction of a programme for teaching mathematics. (It is possible to argue that in a primary school the subject areas should not be considered in isolation; this view is discussed later, in the context of topic planning.)

Approach 1

The headteacher has spent a considerable amount of time examining the maths policy documents of other schools, and has also brought with him a selection of ideas from schools in which he has worked. He edits these selectively to produce a policy for his new school, retaining what he thinks are the best parts from each of the documents he has looked at. He has the finished product duplicated and distributes it at a staff meeting, asking for comments and criticisms at the next meeting.

At the next staff meeting no one says anything detrimental about the policy, and it is agreed that it should be implemented. The head is satisfied that maths in the curriculum is well covered and that there is staff involvement. The documents are proudly shown to colleagues, advisers and a visiting HMI. The head goes on to produce similar 'guidelines' for other subjects.

Critique

This is without doubt the quickest way of producing a policy document. It is also probably the least effective. The head's efforts will have produced a document which takes little account of his new school and makes no allowance for the contributions of colleagues with greater experience in that school.

The lack of dissention at the second staff meeting may have been owing to the reluctance of the staff to dishearten the head in his evident enthusiasm. They may also have recognised the inherent weakness of any consultation process which takes place after the major decisions have been taken. What they were being asked to do was to comment on the fine detail, and their acceptance of the main document was, in a sense, implicit.

Approach 2

The head finds, after reviewing his teachers' responsibilities and expertise, that there is a teacher with responsibility

as maths co-ordinator. The teacher is experienced, knowledgeable and enthusiastic, and responds willingly to the headteacher's request that she draw up a series of maths guidelines which comply with the requirements of the National Curriculum. They agree a deadline for completion.

The process then follows the same pattern as Approach 1, except that the teacher presents the programme to her colleagues. The head, who has commissioned the work, is supportive and approves the final result.

Critique

There is no substantial difference between this approach and Approach 1. The headteacher has merely delegated the work to someone else. The end result may reflect more adequately the particular circumstances of the school, but it is still essentially a one-person effort with all the weaknesses that implies.

Approach 3

The head and his maths co-ordinator discuss the preparation of a policy statement on the teaching of maths in the school. They bear in mind the need to follow the National Curriculum and the importance of being seen by governors and local authority to have a clear statement. The school has recently started using a published maths scheme which, as part of its publicity, emphasises that its use throughout the primary school will deliver the whole National Curriculum in mathematics. The scheme has teachers' handbooks, workbooks, textbooks and work cards.

A statement is prepared which says that the school uses this particular scheme for the teaching of mathematics and which includes extracts from the scheme's handbooks relating to its content and effectiveness.

Critique

This is a common approach to the problem. In a way the head and staff have abdicated their responsibility for curriculum content to a third party, in this case a publisher.

There may be some advantages in this, particularly if the alternative is either no scheme or a poorly constructed one, but the disadvantages are clear. The school has become tied to the use of one particular published scheme and has a financial commitment to its continued use. There is also a danger that the staff will accept the published scheme in its totality without having made a complete assessment of its strengths and weaknesses.

This approach may also suggest that the school staff does not possess sufficient collective expertise to construct a school-based curriculum. The use of a published scheme in this way, with little chance to be selective about content, can have the effect of reducing teachers to operatives who are prevented from exercising professional judgement.

Approach 4
Possibly as a result of encouragement from the headteacher, the staff decide that they need to construct a set of school-based guidelines for the teaching of mathematics, taking into account the school's special circumstances, the LEA and governors' statements on the curriculum and the requirements of the National Curriculum.

They recognise that one or two of the staff have special expertise, but they also realise that, as primary teachers, they will all be involved directly in the teaching of maths and they will each have an interest in what is decided. Under the guidance of the maths co-ordinator, the staff draw up a programme with realistic deadlines which will help them to decide collectively what they want from a maths scheme, and enable them to consider the practical and resource implications, and the form of the end product.

They decide how constraining they want the final document to be, and the degree of scope for professional freedom and flexibility it should contain. After several terms the final version is produced, and it is adopted by the whole staff. It is regularly reviewed in the light of experience and in order to take account of changes in opinions. The scheme uses published material, but teachers are encouraged to be selective about the material they use.

Critique
This approach is time-consuming and difficult to manage, and can lead to a questioning of basic assumptions about curriculum content and methods of delivery. If the aim of the exercise is to get glossy, bound curriculum documents quickly on to the classroom shelves and to satisfy the need to be seen to be doing something, it is not the one to use.

If, on the other hand, you want to use an approach which will go some way towards overcoming the problem of lack of teacher commitment to school guidelines, this may be the way forward. If teachers have been actively involved in the preparation of a document and if it truly represents their views, takes account of their reservations and fears, offers them scope for professional freedom and supports them in their difficulties, they will be willing to give it a try.

Achieving a curriculum policy

The curriculum policy of a primary school must be determined through staff involvement and consultation on a large scale. There must also be an efficient system for regular review.

The headteacher must be prepared and able to delegate to the staff, and even perhaps to some governors, what has previously been seen as her own particular responsibility.

The implications of this are great. The headteacher must recognise the expertise and experience of her staff, and the staff must be interested in and committed to the task in hand. The teachers can no longer expect the job of curriculum formulation to be carried out for them by the headteacher; they must assume part of the responsibility.

The evolution of a plan

Any headteacher needs to recognise that curriculum formulation is a slow process. Rushing it merely reduces the quality of the end product and devalues the efforts of all involved. You and your staff need to evolve a strategic plan which identifies priorities, sets a realistic time-scale, monitors compliance with legislative requirements, details the expertise and resources available and recognises obstacles to change.

It is important that all concerned see the change as both desirable and possible. Above all, the end product must be one in which you and your staff have confidence. This confidence will be transmitted through the teachers to pupils, parents and governors.

Across the curriculum

It is often assumed that the curriculum has to be planned so that traditional subject areas are treated and delivered separately by teachers.

More thoughtful approaches to the implementation of the National Curriculum have led to the conclusion that cross-curricular work is a more positive and practical solution, particularly if the trap of teaching to the attainment targets is to be avoided. Many people believe that the needs of the National Curriculum are best met by the use of an integrated approach.

If we consider for a moment the possible structure of such an integrated approach, it will become clear that it cannot take place without widespread co-operation, consultation and corporate decision-making.

The whole school staff must work together to give a considered response to the following questions:

- What skills, knowledge, attitudes and concepts do we wish to transmit to the children over a broad range of experience?
- How can we ensure that what we present to the children is well matched to their age and ability?
- Is what we are teaching relevant to the children's present experience and to their future lives?
- Have we built in an adequate balance?

If a curriculum plan is approached in this way, the National Curriculum is just one of the criteria taken into account during the process of school-based curriculum design and development.

The questions detailed above should always form part of any consideration of curriculum structure. There is no outrageous conflict between the National Curriculum and a well-planned primary curriculum developed through staff consultation.

Topic-based work

How can a headteacher set about planning for an integrated, school-based, topic-centred approach which at the same time fulfils the requirements of the National Curriculum? The following course of action anticipates some possible pitfalls.

The first task is to decide on the extent and level of topic activity within the school. Is all the work going to be topic-based, or are topics to be used in conjunction with more traditional teaching methods? How many topics a year will a class cover? What proportion of teaching time will be used for topic work?

The answers to these questions, which will depend on the views of those involved and what they hope to achieve, will determine the next course of action. It is at this planning stage that the closest school-wide co-operation and mutual understanding is called for if the exercise is to succeed and benefit the children.

Topics should be chosen collectively, and must take account of the need for the curriculum to be broad, balanced and relevant. Curriculum balance and breadth cannot be assured without consultation and a willingness to consider the whole scope of the curriculum.

The whole staff should be involved in planning the topic work to be undertaken throughout the school during the coming year. You need to arrive at a set of topic activities which each class will cover. The topics chosen for each class must be arrived at by considering which topics have been covered by those children in previous years. You will also have to consider the resources which are available. The decisions should be recorded so that they can be considered again and built upon at the start of the following year. In this way, you will be able to build up an overview of what is going on.

As part of this planning process, you also need to look at each topic to establish which skills and knowledge you intend to transmit through it, and which areas of the curriculum you will cover. At the same time, consider the broader overall package of attitudes and concepts which will be conveyed.

Try to choose topics which can be freely adapted at the detailed planning stage to provide for specific curriculum requirements. Thus a topic on 'the school environment' or 'myself' would be preferable to one on 'famous people' or 'horses': the first two can be extended and developed, with careful planning, to encompass each of the nine principal areas of learning, whereas the latter two present much more limited opportunities for a cross-curricular approach.

There are arguments in favour of a cyclical approach to topic work, where children cover work under the same topic heading on more than one occasion in the primary school years. Children will be able to look at the topic from different aspects at progressively higher levels. Similarly, there is a case for planning a whole-school topic, where a subject such as 'light' is examined from a number of curricular viewpoints simultaneously by all the children in a school.

The possibilities are endless, and there is not room here to examine them in greater detail. The main idea to bear in mind is the need to plan collectively, both across the traditional subject areas and across the age-ranges.

Continuity and progression

An integral part of the planning process, and a key feature of the National Curriculum, is the need to ensure both continuity and progression. These two words are sometimes used almost as if they were interchangeable, but in fact their meanings are quite separate and distinct. Each is an equally important aspect of the education process.

Preserving continuity means ensuring that what is being offered to the children through the curriculum takes account of what has gone before and anticipates what is to come next. Progress, on the other hand, is the way in which children's learning increases and develops through clearly identifiable stages.

The aim should be to identify clearly the areas in which progress is desired, and to optimise this progress by ensuring continuity.

Monitoring and record-keeping

There are many ways in which continuity can be monitored and progress measured, but each requires some form of record-keeping.

You may identify the need to establish an effective record-keeping system as a priority in your school. As with planning the curriculum, you must consider all the options and their relative merits. The starting points will vary from school to school. There may be no system in use, there may be a simple but ineffective system, or the school may have a complex process of record-keeping which you judge to be unworkable.

It is important to begin by establishing a set of aims and objectives, in conjunction with all the staff. You will need to adopt a tactic to channel thought in these initial discussions.

Channelling thought

One technique which has often proved successful is to devise a range of questions which examine basic assumptions and lead to a reappraisal of the existing approach. The first move, therefore, is not to say 'What should we be doing?' but 'What questions should we be asking ourselves?'

The following questions will act as a focus for staff discussion on the introduction of a record-keeping programme.

- Why do you need to record?
- What information do you wish to convey to others through the medium of records?
- What is considered to be a reasonable work-load for the teachers concerned?
- What lessons can be learned from the previous system, or from systems seen in other schools?

It is essential that no record-keeping system is imposed on staff without consultation. The teachers who will have to work the system must be involved in its conception, otherwise they will generate countless obstacles to its effective operation. For more detailed comment on record-keeping, see Chapter 11, 'Keeping a record'.

A special needs policy

The area of special needs can provide a good example of the need to use whole-school planning, cross-curricular balance and meaningful record-keeping in order to produce a relevant school policy.

Most schools want a special needs policy covering the whole age range and involving all teaching staff. Such a policy could be drawn up by the headteacher or by a special needs co-ordinator in isolation, or it could be borrowed from another school, but it is unlikely that either of these approaches would be ideal.

The techniques discussed earlier for involving all staff in the consultation and decision-making process can usefully be applied in this area, as can the method of questioning basic assumptions. The staff must agree on the criteria to be used, on the aims and objectives of the policy, on the overall approach to teaching and on the use of resources – including support teaching if available. It goes without saying that continuity and progress are key aspects of any special needs policy, and the importance of monitoring and record-keeping in this area cannot be too highly stressed.

A School Development Plan

A useful concept which many schools and local authorities have adopted in recent years is that of the School Development Plan. This plan, prepared by the headteacher and staff in consultation with the governors, is usually an annual statement of proposals for developments in specific areas – most commonly curriculum and organisation – together with an analysis of the issues and choices governing such proposals and an outline of methods of implementing them.

The scale of the plan will vary from place to place, but in principle it is thoroughly recommended as a way of focusing attention on the processes of planning and development, and of deciding an order of priority given limited time and resources.

If you have not undertaken such a plan before, it is unlikely that your first one will be a comprehensive statement. The detail contained in each plan and the significance attached to it tend to increase as the years go by and more plans are produced.

An important part of the process is the evaluation of the previous year's statement, and this double perspective – looking back over the successes and failures of the previous years, and speculating and planning for the future – has great advantages.

The plan should be drawn up in consultation with the whole staff, perhaps following a series of staff meetings, or a series of meetings of a working committee who then report back to a full staff meeting.

An example of a standard formula for a plan might be as follows.

1: Evaluation

List the aims of the previous year's plan if any, and then give an evaluation of work directed at achieving those aims. Comment on successes and failures. Consider the content and implementation of last year's plan point by point.

2: Aims for the first year

List the aims for the first year of the new plan. (The development plan may cover a number of years. The first year should be planned in great detail; the aims for subsequent years will be amended as time progresses.)

The following are some possible aims:

- To develop further the involvement of teachers in curriculum leadership;
- To work towards involving all staff in curriculum and school organisation;
- To continue the process of codifying the practice and procedures agreed among staff, in order to support induction;
- To continue the process of curriculum review and update.

3: Specific objectives for the first year

This section should include details of specific proposals and programmes of work designed to achieve the aims you have decided on for the year; for example:

- To develop a whole-school programme of study for religious education;
- To develop and introduce a programme for 'education for personal relationships';

• To consider the approach to topic work in the school;
• To extend the home reading scheme;
• To continue the special needs programme.

Detail the training implications of your objectives, and any likely whole-staff absence for INSET days – give the dates.

4: Analysis
Give an analysis of the issues involved in deciding on the objectives for the plan. Why were certain priorities highlighted? What difficulties are expected?

5: Implementation
How is the plan to be implemented? How will the objectives be met? List the courses of action by which you will achieve your objectives; for example:
• The continued release of curriculum leaders, on a regular basis, to attend courses to improve leadership and management skills as well as individual subject expertise;
• The continuation of working groups established during the year;
• Holding more staff-led workshops for colleagues in specific curriculum areas;
• The holding of an annual meeting to discuss and agree financial priorities for the use of official and private funds.

Give details of the likely effects of your proposals upon finances, staffing and resources.

6: Long-term plans
Provide information about any longer-term plans.

The advantages of a plan
The principal advantages of a School Development Plan are as follows:
• It calls for collective discussion and agreement on a number of key issues.
• It provides a focus of attention.
• It generates courses of action.
• It creates a working time-scale.
• It has a built-in opportunity for review and evaluation.

The development plan is valuable in curriculum design, review and assessment.

Differing perspectives

One final point to emphasise on the issue of curriculum planning is that each school can have three curricula, or at least three distinct perspectives on one curriculum.

There is the curriculum as planned (whether by an individual or as the consequence of a corporate planning procedure), the curriculum as delivered by the teacher or teaching team, and the curriculum as received by the child. These variations in perspective can make a great difference. It is rather like viewing a piece of sculpture from three different angles; each viewpoint offers different opportunities for interpretation. The ideal is to work towards the closest possible harmony between what is planned, what is delivered and what is received. This can only be achieved through a high level of co-operation and consultation.

Perhaps the most significant role of the headteacher is in the area of curriculum planning and development. As in so many aspects of the headteacher's role, the difference between success and failure is often a result of the degree of planning, the level of staff involvement, the timing, and above all the headteacher's own expertise and enthusiasm.

Chapter Eight

Relations with the office

When considering the headteacher's contact with the Education Department it is important to understand the fundamental difference in perspective between those working in school and those working in 'the office'. This different perspective gives rise to varying priorities and attitudes.

Different headteachers have a variety of attitudes towards the Education Department, ranging from reverence to disdain. It is better to take a middle line which recognises the contribution which the Local Authority and its officers make to your work, while basing your own actions largely on school-based criteria.

Finding out who does what

As a new headteacher, you will be faced with a list of names and telephone numbers of people who work in the Education Office. You need to find out fairly rapidly who does what and, more importantly, who to contact for the help you want and the things you need.

There will, of course, be a hierarchy, but it may not always be the person at the top who will be of most help. Sometimes going to the top can get things done most rapidly, but at other times you may find that someone a little lower down the ladder has the information or the resources you need.

It certainly takes a while to sort out the names and personalities in the Education Department, but once you have done it, you know who to go to quickly should an urgent need arise.

Because of the wide variation in size and organisation of different Local Authorities it is impossible to give a detailed plan of who does what. In some parts of the country decisions about aspects of individual school staffing or finance have to be taken at the highest level, whereas in other areas relatively junior staff have wide-ranging delegated powers and discretion.

You need to distinguish between administrative (or officer) staff, and professional (or advisory) staff. They have quite distinct roles, and raising the wrong type of question with them is a waste of time.

Generally speaking, administrative staff deal with matters connected with the day-to-day running of schools — staffing, finance, premises, equipment, lettings, governors, pupil numbers, welfare — while advisory staff are concerned with the curriculum, assessment and the professional development of teaching staff. There may be some overlap in certain areas — for example, interviewing and appointment of teaching staff — and you should establish what the local practice is, but as a rule these roles are quite separate.

Administrative staff

Increasingly, officers are concerned with the administration and support of schools involved in LMS, and the expertise and experience which they are able to bring to specific problems in this field is invaluable.

When dealing with the Education Department, whether in respect of staffing, finance, equipment or any other matter, don't assume that there is no room for negotiation. If, for instance, you need more resources than are on offer, it is worth trying to negotiate for them. Often there is something kept in reserve, of which you may be able to obtain a share. Deciding how far you can travel along this path is a matter of experience and of knowing your people. You don't hurt anyone by asking.

The role of many officers has changed significantly with the advent of LMS, and they are now less frequently involved in the direct allocation of resources to schools. This is because of the delegation of large areas of expenditure to the governing bodies of individual schools.

There may be occasions when help has to be sought from the office in respect of specific resources or funding which is not covered by the delegated budget. When such an approach is necessary, you should be clear about what you are requesting and what your supporting argument is. If possible, it can be an advantage to assemble all the facts in the form of a bid or submission. In this way there is less risk of ambiguity.

Advisers

The other representatives of the Local Authority with whom schools and particularly headteachers come into regular contact are the advisers. Advisers are quite distinct from officers in that they have almost invariably had some teaching experience. Most subject advisers have a secondary background, whereas specialist primary advisers have usually been primary headteachers.

Teachers as a group are generally sceptical of people who try to tell them how to do their job, unless there is evidence that those people have experience of doing it in a better way, and unless the advice is capable of being implemented in the average overcrowded, under-resourced classroom.

Because of this scepticism, advisers often receive a mixed reception. This problem is compounded by the fact that in some Local Authority areas advisers are known as inspectors. The difference in title may be a historical accident without significance, but most people would rather receive advice than be the subject of an inspection.

The role of the advisers or inspectors varies from area to area, depending on the attitude of the Local Authority they represent. Some authorities employ inspectors whose role is principally one of appraisal and assessment. In other authorities the advisers have a consultancy role and are not, except in extreme circumstances, concerned with assessment in relation to individual schools. The latter system makes it more possible for advisers and schools to work together in a co-operative way and with mutual trust.

There can be a fruitful relationship between headteacher and adviser if a pattern of mutual understanding and respect is developed. The best working relationships arise where the headteacher actively seeks the assistance of an adviser, and where the adviser is able to offer genuine and constructive help, and to follow this up with some tangible support.

It is important that the adviser is not seen by staff as someone to whom only the head talks, and who is never involved with the teachers or the children. If advice is practical and constructive it is usually welcomed by teachers, and many examples of good practice can be transmitted through the medium of the advisory service.

Advisers can be extremely useful to headteachers, particularly when they have been headteachers themselves. It is important to remember, though, that they will rarely solve problems for you or take direct action. More often they will offer a range of advice, a sounding board for ideas, or possibly some extra resources or money. In the end it is you who have to make the decisions and take action, and of course you take the responsibility if things go wrong and the credit when things work out. You are not obliged to seek advice, or to take it if you feel it is not sound, but often an additional point of view helps you to decide which course to take.

The arrival of the National Curriculum has meant that Local Authorities are required to satisfy themselves and others that certain standards are being maintained in schools. Handled well, this sort of appraisal can be a beneficial and positive process. Handled badly, it can breed discontent and reduce morale among the teaching staff.

If criticisms arise from the Local Authority as a result of an inspection, and if these are related to resources, facilities, staffing or lack of training, then the problems should be solved by additional provision. If a need for extra training is implied, then this too should be provided. Teachers and headteachers should try to view inspection as a positive step towards greater provision for their needs and greater recognition of their problems and difficulties.

The role of the LEA

Following the advent of Local Management of Schools, local authorities are finding some of their traditional roles under threat. In the past, a school's every need was met by the LEA. Depending on the degree of support, guidance and resources provided by the LEA, the schools either prospered and did well, or were under-resourced and fared badly.

With LMS the situation has changed. Increasingly the officers of the authority are taking on the role of offering advice and services which schools are free to accept or reject in favour of other sources. This change has brought market forces into what has always been a rather cosy love-hate relationship between schools and 'office'.

Assessing priorities

As a headteacher, surrounded by immediate and apparently pressing demands, one can come to regard the activities of the Local Authority with undue and excessive reverence. It is sometimes tempting to give them a disproportionate

amount of time, possibly to the detriment of the school, children and staff. It is a good idea to keep one's priorities in order by asking some simple questions:

- What will happen if I don't do this today?
- What will happen if I never do this?
- How important is it to me and the school that this gets done?
- Will doing this stop me doing something which I feel is more important?
- Is there a simpler way of achieving the same result?

If you apply these criteria to the range of forms and requests for action which arrive weekly from the average Education Department, you should soon reach a satisfactory working relationship.

You are responsible for the school, and you and your staff know more than the Education Department do about the factors which affect the running of the school. You should never be prevented from doing what you think is right for the school, the children and the staff simply because of constraints placed on you by an LEA.

This is not intended as an incitement to disobedience, but it is the headteacher, after all, who has a legal responsibility to the governors for the day-to-day running of the school. It is the headteacher, too, who is ultimately responsible for taking action to solve any problems which may arise.

Getting things done

Just sometimes, a philosophy of taking action first and asking permission afterwards pays dividends. If you want to take an unusual course of action which you think is in the best interests of the school it can be very frustrating to seek permission in advance from the authority, particularly if you need to take the action quickly. You may be told that it cannot be done, or that it will have to be referred to someone else and you will have to wait for a decision. This may mean a missed opportunity.

It can be quite different if you decide to carry out the action and inform the 'office' afterwards. The person you deal with may be relieved at not having to make the decision and may merely acknowledge your information. Or you may get no response at all.

Deciding which approach to adopt is something that becomes easier with experience and confidence, but any headteacher has to think of the outcome when considering possible courses of action. If as an experienced professional you think that what you propose is right, and if you are prepared to stand by your decision and its consequences, then you should not be prevented from taking that course of action. As a profession, the more we are prepared to defer to others on decisions which are rightly ours, the more we weaken our status.

There will probably be many occasions, however, on which the experience of the Local Authority officers will be invaluable to you. You must exercise your own professional judgement over the matters which you refer to them, in order to use their skills and knowledge in the best possible way.

Chapter Nine

Making ends meet

During my first headship, in a voluntary aided church school, a regular annual item on the agenda of the governors' meeting was 'School's private fund account, headteacher to report'. I used to ask one of my staff to audit the school fund books a few weeks before, so that I could produce a statement and balance sheet at the meeting, for my governors to read and agree.

It happened that in this school, as a result of some historic arrangement, the chief education officer acted as clerk to the governors. Since he was obviously a busy man, he used to send one of his officers in his place, to represent him at the meeting.

I had at that time a firm conviction (which was fortunately supported by the chairman of the governors) that the Local Authority had no right to see, inspect or know about the school's private account. I was quite sure that I was accountable only to the governors on this matter.

The chief education officer's representative, however, did not support this view.

The meeting when the accounts were presented was notable because every year, at some stage in the proceedings, there would ensue a sort of dignified tug-of-war involving the clerk and either myself or the chairman. The clerk's object would be to get hold of a copy of the balance sheet and whip it back to the borough treasurer as soon as possible. Our aim would be to prevent him from carrying out his objective, and to ensure that the bank balance remained a secret shared only by the governors.

We had a point to make, based on our belief that certain matters of school finance were not the concern of the Local Authority. The borough treasurer certainly had a right to know that the school's accounts had been properly audited, but the governors and I had a number of reasons for not wanting him to know the details of the private funds we had at our disposal.

Our reasons were nothing to do with dishonesty or sharp practice, but stemmed from our concern that if an authority came to think of particular schools as being 'wealthy' as a result of parental donations or fund-raising activities, this might have an influence upon their decisions about the allocation of official money between the schools in their area.

This story illustrates the distinction between the various sources of money which headteachers – or more correctly governors – have at their disposal for use in school. The governors now have an overall responsibility for the spending of official funds (capitation). Even in small schools, which may not be eligible for inclusion in the main schemes, the introduction of LMS has added considerably to the financial responsibilities of the governors.

Governors and financial delegation

Governors have long had a right to know about private funds. More recently, however, they have acquired extra rights in respect of the spending of official money.

As a result of the Education Reform Act of 1988, local management schemes have increased governors' financial responsibilities. The associated administrative and accountancy work has inevitably increased to keep pace with this.

In some schools there may be governors who are able and willing to accept an increased share of the administrative burden. Some may even be able to offer their schools some professional advice on money management. In other schools, however, it is likely that the headteacher and staff will have to take on most of the additional responsibility.

This chapter looks at some aspects of managing finances in a primary school, and considers some of the associated problems. It also offers some suggestions for developing new tactics, relating these to the broader issues of LMS.

Rules and conditions vary greatly from authority to authority, particularly in the way LMS schemes are operated, and for this reason some of the suggestions given here may not be practical in certain areas. In addition, some LEAs are of course more liberal than others, and may already have introduced reforms far more wide-ranging than these suggestions.

The use of public funds under LMS

Local Management of Schools was a direct consequence of the Education Reform Act of 1988. This meant that every school with over 200 pupils should be included in a scheme drawn up by the Local Educational Authority in accordance with government guidelines. The scheme meant that the school governors became directly responsible for significant aspects of school finances, personnel and premises. In practice, many local authorities chose to include smaller schools as well in the delegated budget proposals.

The ways in which the money available is distributed by the Local Authority to each school are strictly prescribed by the Act, so that the concept of a budget share based upon 'formula funding' replaces any previous budget which particular schools may have received. The number and ages of the children on roll will determine 75 per cent of the budget for each school, and the remaining amount can be varied to take account of other specified circumstances, such as children with special needs, the quality and type of premises and the school's catchment area.

The budget share is based on the Aggregated Schools Budget. This is determined by the legislation, and the items which a Local Education Authority may not include, or which it can choose not to include (Mandatory and Discretionary Exceptions) are severely limited.

The total sum allocated to the governors of your school by the authority in this way has to be budgeted in consultation with the headteacher, to cover the various expenditure headings — staff costs, premises maintenance, books and equipment, heating and lighting — and the range of other items for which they are responsible. Many governing bodies have separate finance committees to deal with this issue.

Staffing costs

Many would argue that the quantity and quality of the teaching and non-teaching staff employed is the key factor in determining the effectiveness and efficiency of a school. The cost of staffing certainly makes up by far the greatest part of the expenditure of individual schools. Most primary school governors have discovered that staffing costs amount to more than 80 per cent of their delegated budgets. When deciding on the use of delegated funds for staffing, the following factors should be considered:

- The difference in numbers between teaching and non-teaching staff;
- The number of staff necessary in each category given the roll of the school, any relevant special circumstances, and the headteacher's and governors' policy on the curriculum;
- The qualifications and seniority of teaching staff currently employed;
- The allocation of above-scale incentive allowances within the school.

Decisions in each of these areas will help determine the use of available resources.

Teaching staff

The number of teaching staff employed will be related primarily to the number of children on roll. This figure should not be too different from that produced by the LEA's staffing formula under the previous budget. The major area of concern is the age and experience of the teaching staff employed. There is a regulation applying to LMS schemes which explicitly requires that budget shares should not be varied to allow for differences in salary costs between employing teachers relatively lower or higher on the salary scales, or to take into account incremental drift. The actual costs of employing each teacher therefore have to be taken into account by governing bodies when setting their budgets and considering their staffing costs. Some teachers will be cheaper to employ than others, and in some circumstances governors may only be able to employ younger, more recently qualified teachers.

Management structures in primary schools are generally considered in terms of the range and level of incentive allowances available. LMS removes from governors many of the previous restrictions on the number and level of allowances which can be offered, but there are financial constraints. Although governors may find it an attractive proposition to create a management structure comprising 'C's, 'B's and 'A's — and the headteacher's advice ought to be sought in this respect — they may be constrained from doing so by the cost of existing staffing levels.

Headteachers and governors who are considering the staffing structures of their school need to consider very carefully the age and experience of their staff, and to anticipate the increased staffing costs which will result automatically from incremental drift.

Staffing structures should preferably be planned over a cycle of a number of years, in order to allow for school and personal development. Local Authority officers are experienced in undertaking exercises like this on a much larger scale and it is important to seek and heed their advice.

You must also allow for contingencies — depending on what provisions have been made in your LEA's plan — so that unforeseen long-term absences and maternity leave may be covered without disrupting the overall planning strategy.

Non-teaching staff

All these points apply equally to non-teaching staff. You need to try to achieve a balance between a viable and effective level of teaching staff and an adequate staff of support personnel.

Premises

The involvement of headteachers and their governors with the management of premises under LMS varies considerably according to a range of circumstances. It is not possible to generalise. However, it is sensible to anticipate a few of the problems which may arise.

The ground rules of LMS limit the allowance given to the idiosyncrasies of school buildings when determining budget share. But all Local Authorities have been able, within the restrictions, to take some account of the type, size and age of school buildings.

The main areas to consider in respect of premises are:

- Repairs to and maintenance of the external fabric of the building;
- Repairs to and maintenance of the interior of the building;
- General upkeep and cleaning;
- Use of the premises by outside agencies;
- Costs involved in using the building — heating, lighting, rates and so on.

Many LEAs have arranged insurance or support schemes which cover certain repairs and capital projects. These vary a great deal and, in some cases, governors are offered a range of options which they can elect to join. Typically, the LEA offers various degrees of agency service relating to architects or surveyors or maintenance work — sometimes including internal and external redecoration — which governing bodies can buy into, using an agreed proportion of the delegated budget. These options, where they exist, should be considered very carefully.

As in the case of staffing, it is advisable to seek the advice of Local Authority officers wherever possible, and to draw on their wide experience.

Savings may be achieved in the running costs of the school. It is often the case that promotion of a more careful use of heating, lighting and disposable resources can result in great savings.

Books and equipment

The agreed proportion of the budget share which is set aside to cover the purchase of books and equipment may correspond largely with the old capitation allowance in terms of the items for which it is intended to provide. The sum may, of course, be higher or lower under LMS than it was before. Although practice will vary from area to area, responsibility for this aspect of expenditure may well be delegated to the headteacher.

It is likely, too, that the agreed sum will be made available from the start of the financial year. However, the headteacher will be concerned largely with planning for the next school year which begins five months later. As headteacher you need to look at the whole sum available and to assess, ideally with the help of senior colleagues, the areas to which money needs to be allocated. Then you will be able to arrive at a figure for each area.

Planning your expenditure

In planning for any school year there will be certain items for which the costs remain more or less constant. Telephone bills, television licences and routine equipment maintenance tend to be relatively predictable costs and it is a straightforward process to deduct these from the total.

You may be able to economise a little on items such as office and classroom stationery, but the costs will be fairly constant and can therefore be anticipated and planned for.

Once these constant and predictable items have been removed from the total, a balance is left from which it is advisable to deduct a contingency sum. The amount to deduct is best decided on through experience. Contingency sums are not often estimated correctly, since by definition they exist to cover the unplanned and unforeseen. At least LMS allows savings to be carried forward into the next financial year. If you wish, amounts from the contingency sum may be released gradually for use in other ways as the year progresses.

What is left after all these deductions is the working money, out of which you will have to provide for all the curriculum needs of the school. The same money may also have to pay for furniture, educational visits and other items.

Allocating the money

It is at this stage that the difficult decisions start to arise. How do you decide the amount to be spent in each area? How do you arrive at priorities? What should you use as criteria for determining the amounts to be allocated?

Some of the questions may be answered in part by your circumstances. Some activities tend to be more expensive than others. If you use a maths or language scheme which requires the purchase of disposable workbooks, this will have an immediate effect on your level of expenditure.

At some stage in this procedure you will arrive at a sum of money, small or large, which is available for division among the various curricular and activity areas. You have two decisions to make about this:

- How are you going to arrive at the proportions allocated to each area?
- Having resolved this question, how are you going to plan the spending of the money usefully and effectively?

If you have a routine of staff consultation, an established structure of curriculum co-ordinators and a management team, answering these questions will be far easier than if you have to arrive at a solution by yourself. There may however be some short-term advantages – such as saving time and avoiding possible disagreement – in making the decision yourself, providing you are prepared to live with the longer-term consequence of staff dissatisfaction.

No matter how the money is divided, someone will feel that their subject or age-group should have received more. If the decision is arrived at collectively, the rationale behind it can at least be examined and questioned by all concerned.

There are many ways of dividing 'capitation'.

Immediate need

Some headteachers don't bother with any division, but simply allocate money throughout the year on the basis of immediate need. If, in April, a new set of language workbooks is required, then money is allocated. If one month later several classes need stationery then that is ordered, and so on.

No doubt those who operate such a system find it works for them, but there are immense drawbacks in terms of planning and ensuring a fair allocation of limited resources across a balanced, broad curriculum.

Class or year group

Another popular way of distributing funds is to do it on a class or year group basis. Each class teacher or group of teachers has a sum which they can use individually or jointly for the benefit of the children in their charge. Although this system is plainly fair at the individual level — no teacher has any more to spend than any other — it overlooks the variations in need which arise in the course of certain activities with particular classes and age groups. It also precludes the possibility of spending a lot of money on one school project — say a large amount of centrally stored science equipment.

The biggest disadvantage of this approach is that it reduces the opportunities for whole-school planning and moves teachers towards an egocentric, class-based approach. Given a sum of money to spend on a class, most teachers will immediately look for something to spend it on, even if there is no pressing need. In this way it is easy for them to overlook the more pressing needs of others.

Subject or curriculum

Another way of allocating money is to adopt a subject- or curriculum-based approach, and to allocate money in

various proportions to a list of curriculum areas determined in advance. The two decisions which have to be made here are firstly the areas to which money is to be allocated, and secondly the proportions in which it is to be allocated. Neither of these decisions should be made by the headteacher alone.

The first of the decisions is related to the concept of school curriculum organisation which the headteacher and staff share. The curriculum may be divided into traditional subject areas such as mathematics, PE and science, or it may be related to topics. It could also be seen in terms of age groups; lower school, middle school and upper school. The first of these approaches is by far the most common, and it does allow expenditure in each area to be identified more easily. It is probable that each subject area is led by a specific teacher to whom it would be possible to delegate all or part of the expenditure.

The second decision, relating to the proportion of money allocated to each area, can be more contentious. At first sight it might seem a good idea to divide the available money evenly among the areas, but this can cause problems.

Some curriculum activities may, by their nature, cost more than others. They may require the use of more expensive equipment, or they may normally be associated with the use of disposable workbooks. In some schools there may be a need to spend more in one subject area to compensate for a shortfall in the past.

Collective decision-making

As headteacher, you have an overall perspective on this situation, but you may not see the whole picture in detail. The true state of affairs may be concealed by your own prejudices, by the modesty of some teachers in stating their case for more resources, by the resourcefulness of other teachers in making good, efficient use of limited facilities, or by the forcefulness of others' demands.

For this reason it is essential that decisions about allocations are made collectively and that all concerned have the chance to voice their opinions and reservations about what is proposed. If teachers are involved in the decisions about allocations, see the amounts of money involved and then have to undertake the exercise of providing all that is needed within the given budget, they will be more selective in their choice of materials and also more willing to economise where appropriate.

It is useful to think in terms of percentages at this stage rather than sums of money. It is easier to compare one year's expenditure with the next in this way, and it is also easier for the staff who are considering the distribution of money to remain objective about the process if they have no prior knowledge of the actual amounts of money involved.

You will probably need a series of meetings to decide the percentage allocations to each area. It is at this stage that individual teachers or interest groups within the school have the chance to make their representations and mount campaigns in favour of their areas. As everything takes place in an open meeting, there will be fewer opportunities for charges of unfairness or favouritism, and the end result should be reached by consensus. You may even find that teachers who are well provided-for actually sacrifice part of their allocation in favour of a less generously funded colleague. It can be a good unifying exercise.

As with all decision-making processes carried out at meetings, you have to know your staff. Guard against the more forceful members dominating proceedings and getting their own way. You must protect the less forceful and ensure that the overall balance of the end result is about right in your view. In this respect there is nothing wrong with the head-teacher having a preconceived notion of a fair balance and going to the meeting with this in mind.

This open meeting technique is helpful in developing a team approach to financial management, and can readily be extended into other areas. Sensible decisions about the allocation of funds to various curriculum areas will depend on your consideration of the relative merits of those areas, and upon a review of practice and procedure. If all staff are involved in these stages they will tend to develop a whole-school attitude, and will be less likely to view their own needs in isolation.

Consulting the governors

Even if the 'capitation' spending has been delegated to the headteacher and staff, governors still need to be fitted into the decision-making process. They should be consulted, and they must be asked to approve the final budget. They may wish to question certain decisions, so you and your staff must be prepared and able to justify particular courses of action. This is another important reason for corporate decision-making and for collective responsibility for the decisions. If the teachers are not united in what they want and cannot agree upon or justify a form of spending, there is little hope of the governors accepting it. The governors will be more likely to reduce the delegated responsibility in future.

Where trust and common sense are lacking, the situation can become difficult and good curriculum management may break down for lack of appropriate resources. There is nothing new in the idea of expenditure by professionals being monitored by a lay body. Teachers should try to view it as a positive step towards greater independence and freedom within schools and away from centralisation of funding and decision making. With luck, governors will pitch their intervention at the right level and be seen as allies and colleagues.

What has been described so far is essentially a hierarchical financial management structure for the use of 'official' funds, starting with the LEA which makes the money available to the governors, who then delegate all or part of the responsibility for spending it to the headteacher. The headteacher then consults and co-operates with the staff to decide on the most effective way of dividing and spending the money for the benefit of the children.

If everyone is involved in the process in this way, all will share the responsibility for the careful use of money, and all will feel a greater sense of commitment towards the school and the use of resources.

Private funds

This chapter began by describing a battle over information about private funds. Much of what has been said about public funds can be applied equally to the spending of private funds. However, in many schools private funds have taken on a special status, so we need to take a careful look at the issues surrounding their acquisition and use.

It is important to remember that money from private sources may have been given to support particular areas of expenditure, or that there may be a strongly-held view among the staff or parents that private money should not be used for 'essential' items. You need to consider these viewpoints and to be aware of them in any money management policy.

Private funds in schools can come from a variety of sources. Parents' associations may donate money for specific projects, or may make a block grant for general use in the school at the headteacher's discretion. There may be school-based fund-raising activities, or there may be income from various types of sponsorship or enterprise, such as the sale of school photographs or uniforms.

Each of these sources yields revenue which may or may not be earmarked for specific projects, and the headteacher has a responsibility to the governors for its management. It is important to ensure that all the money is carefully accounted for and that you are scrupulous in its disposal. When dealing with money in school, a useful maxim to remember is 'Public money is publicly accountable, private money is privately accountable'.

As far as public money is concerned, you can rely on the Internal Audit Department to monitor your accounting, but in the private sector accountability may be less thorough. For this reason, you need to impose your own system, both to safeguard your own position and to ensure the integrity of the school in relation to those who have given the money.

In respect of private funds the headteacher is accountable to the governors and should report regularly — at the very minimum annually — on the state of any bank accounts and the disposal of any private income. The Local Authority has no role in this process, except perhaps to ensure that it occurs and that accounts are properly audited.

Private fund or school fund accounts can be a source of a sizeable income to some schools and can offer great flexibility to headteachers. It is possible to invest the money in deposit accounts and thereby to overcome, at least to some extent, the tyranny of the financial year.

The prospect of financial management can be daunting, but sharing the burden of responsibility with staff and with governors can have many unanticipated advantages. A headteacher who has entered the era of LMS with the help of a financial management team can look forward to greater freedom and opportunity to develop the school and the curriculum than ever before.

Chapter Ten

Working with parents

Teachers and headteachers vary enormously in their attitudes to parents. In some schools parents are welcomed, involved in classroom activities, invited to school functions and generally helped to participate in the life of the school; in others they are viewed almost with suspicion. No doubt there are reasons for these wide differences in approach, but most schools manage to steer a middle course between the two extremes.

The aim of this chapter is to question some of the attitudes towards parents and the assumptions which are made about them, so that you can arrive at a reasoned decision about the best approach to adopt, given the circumstances in which you find yourself.

How do we think of parents?

Traditionally, parents have been seen as the providers of the raw materials of education. This attitude has tended to give them a fairly low status and consequently little say in the process of education. In this respect a headteacher is rather like a manufacturer or factory owner, who only attaches importance to the supplier of raw materials when supply is short. At other times, all his or her attention goes into the manufacturing process rather than the source of the materials.

Now, however, the traditional view of parents in education is being challenged, and it is recognised that there are various different roles they can play in the educational system.

Parents as clients

One way of considering parents is to think of them as clients. The parents are part of a professional partnership, rather like that which exists between a doctor and his patient, or between a solicitor and her client.

This approach affords greater respect to the parents, but it also tends to minimise the competition which goes on between schools with the intention of attracting parents. The assumption at the basis of this type of relationship is that the professionals know best and that their judgements and decisions cannot be questioned - or at any rate, not without involving the client in a lengthy and difficult search for a second opinion.

Parents as customers

Recent government legislation has endeavoured to increase parental choice and involvement in education, and this aspect of educational reform has received plenty of publicity. This means that schools now have to promote themselves in the attempt to attract parents, rather than simply offering a service on a 'take it or leave it' basis.

This move towards greater competition, while it is in line with government philosophies in other areas, introduces a number of difficulties into school management which headteachers will have to resolve. One approach is to regard parents as customers who are paying for a service and who have the right to take their business elsewhere if dissatisfied. This high-street approach to education seems in some ways to remove professional judgement from headteachers and teachers, replacing it with the notion of customer choice and quality of service.

The degree to which this approach is adopted depends on a number of factors, not least the extent to which the school is over- or under-subscribed. A popular school with parents clamouring for places is less likely to be influenced by market forces than one in which there are half-empty classrooms. Some might argue that the popular school is full because it is offering the type of service which parents want, but matters are not always that simple and other factors should be considered.

The idea that 'the customer is always right' as applied to education is one which most teachers view with horror, and which is largely incompatible with accepted practice to date. However, it is growing, and headteachers and schools have to come to terms with it and try to reconcile it with a professional approach to education.

Knowing your customers

Above all, the headteacher needs to build a relationship of trust with parents. They must come to respect his professional ability and that of the teaching staff, and in this way a successful partnership will develop. Parents, like staff, may be suspicious of a new head. They may wonder what changes there will be and whether a new regime may damage their child's education.

The key rules to remember are to be sure of your own ideas, to appear confident about them (without seeming arrogant) and to take care to avoid too much rapid and radical change at an early stage.

Parents in school

There was a time when parents were discouraged from entering schools for any reason. Children were left at the gate and teachers took over from that point. Any contact was a rarity, and most communication took the form of letters and written reports.

Fortunately, this has now changed. These days parental involvement in schools is widespread. It takes four distinct forms, any one of which headteachers can encourage by their attitude and by the relationships they build. Some difficulties may arise because of the different roles parents play in each form of involvement, and you should be conscious of the need for subtle variations in your approach in each case.

Parental consultation

Perhaps the most obvious, and certainly the most important type of parental involvement with schools, is that which develops between school staff and parents in respect of individual children. Three questions arise in connection with this:

- What system of communication and consultation exists within the school to ensure that information about the progress of individual children is passed on?
- How are parents informed about what is happening to their children?
- What opportunities do class teachers have to find out more about the children they teach from the parents — the people who know them best?

You can use these questions to examine and review the parental consultation procedure in use in your school. The aim is to reach a compromise which will give parents the best possible service, without overloading the teachers and diverting them from their principal role as educators.

If the school's tradition has been to hold one parents' evening a year, during which parents jostle for the privilege of a five-minute chat with the teacher in the corner of a crowded classroom, think about reviewing the system. What does this arrangement contribute to the welfare and education of the children? What does it contribute to the dignity of their parents and the professional status of the teachers? Is there a better way of achieving what is required?

In order to answer this last question satisfactorily you and your staff must reach an agreement on what parents' evenings are intended to achieve. As a public relations exercise many traditional parents' evenings fail dismally. If the meetings are intended for exchanging significant information about individual children, the 'five-minute rush' is probably not the best approach.

Individual schools must make their own arrangements to suit their own circumstances and the needs of both parents and staff, but some factors are common to all. The following is a list of suggested approaches which, if used selectively, may provide headteachers with a range of strategies for developing the parental consultation process to meet the needs of the present day.

Parents' evenings

If you use parents' evenings, consider the time of year at which they are held. Is late in the summer term the most effective time if the class teacher is proposing any form of review or remedial action as a result of the meeting? The middle of the autumn or spring term may be more suitable.

Think about the mechanics of your parents' evenings. Do you set a date or dates and expect parents to fight it out on a first come, first served basis? Do you offer general time-slots or specific appointments? How good are your staff at sticking to the appointments once they have been arranged? If individual teachers are left to arrange their own appointments, how do you co-ordinate things when you have more than one child from the same family in the school?

The type of arrangement made for formal parents' evenings depends on a great many things. Most important is the size of the school, the number of children in each class and the importance teachers place upon the activity. If teachers see communication of this sort as useful to their professional duties they will be willing to make extra time available. If they view it as an annual penance which tells them nothing they did not already know, they will be less enthusiastic.

Consultation day

Regular consultation days have been set up successfully in many schools. This arrangement ensures that teachers are available on a certain day of each week, possibly on a rota basis, to see parents either with or without an appointment. It has a number of advantages:

- It reduces the pressure on the formal annual or termly meetings.
- It offers parents the chance to seek advice and information from teachers as they feel the need, without having to wait for formal invitations and without having to take the difficult step of making special arrangements to approach the school or teacher on a matter of concern.
- It gives teachers the chance to build a more rounded picture of individual children than they could from parents' evenings alone.
- Perhaps the biggest single advantage of the weekly 'surgery' is that it becomes a custom, so both teachers and parents get used to it and find nothing strange in talking to each other on these occasions.

Any process which reduces the level of formality, building mutual trust and respect and improving the flow of information, must be beneficial. Such an arrangement can, of course, be either a supplement to or a substitute for the traditional formal evenings.

Reports

Some schools have an established practice of sending home termly, twice-yearly or annual written reports. Some form of written comment on a child is welcomed by most parents, and it often provides a valuable support for the activities of parents' evenings. However, careful thought should be given to the form the reports should take and the level of guidance which should be offered to teachers before they complete them.

Casual comments written by a teacher in a report are open to misinterpretation and misunderstanding, and may well seem of greater significance than a verbal remark. Parents sometimes make much of the variations which occur from year to year in what is said about their children by different teachers, so a degree of standardisation and moderation is advisable.

If, for example, successive teachers have given the parents of a particular child no reason to feel concerned about his or her progress or behaviour, then suddenly one teacher makes significant and detrimental comments about it, the parents will feel entitled to express concern about variations in professional judgement. You should always see each written report, and it may also be a good idea to countersign the reports before they are sent to the parents. In this way some problems may be avoided, and you will also be forewarned about possible trouble-spots.

Parents as governors

The development of the role of parent governors has been seen by some as an important step towards increasing the accountability of schools, headteachers and teachers to their 'clients'.

It is important for both the headteacher and the parent concerned to understand that a parent governor has exactly the same rights and responsibilities as any other governor, and is subject to the same protocol and ethics. They are not delegates, but governors in their own right, free to take actions and make decisions according to their own judgement within the constitution of the governing body, although they should be mindful of the parent group they represent.

Difficulties can arise when a parent is active in school in a number of roles, for example as a parent governor and as a voluntary helper. In this situation you, as headteacher, must be clear about the terms on which you are discussing matters. Nothing should interfere with the professional relationship you have with the parent of a child in your care, even the fact that the parent is also a governor.

Parents working in school

In many schools these days it is common to see parents working alongside children and teachers, both in and out of the classrooms. The range of activities in which they can be involved is huge. In such schools parents are welcomed as partners and as valuable extra helpers, as they can enable the school to offer greater facilities to the children.

What is often overlooked by observers is that these working relationships have usually evolved over a number of years. They will have developed gradually, through a process of learning from mistakes, taking account of good and bad practice, building on individual strengths and talents and reinforcing mutual confidence. It is rare that such a relationship is established rapidly; if it is, the end result may well be unsatisfactory.

If yours is a school in which there is a great deal of parental activity, you are in many ways extremely lucky, and you need only ask yourself two questions.

• Are you satisfied that all the teachers who are working in partnership with parents are happy with the arrangement?
• Are all the activities which the parents undertake of a type appropriate for untrained volunteer helpers?

If the answers to these questions are satisfactory, then the way is open for further developments.

If you find yourself in a school where parents are not involved, or have only a limited involvement, the process is more difficult.

The best approach in this case is a gradual increase in involvement, starting with ancillary help outside the classroom — with libraries, for example — and then moving on to involve any teachers who have expressed an active interest in using volunteer help. By this means parents will become a more common and acceptable sight in and around the school, and it should become clear how valuable their efforts can be.

By using a gradual approach you will be able to see which parents are most useful and which, if any, need to be discouraged. You must be sure that the helpers are responsible, helpful people to have in the classroom. Those parents who are not so good working directly with children can be gradually moved away from direct contact and redeployed on other, more routine tasks. Always remember to be tactful in situations like this.

There is no doubt that parents will occasionally use this route to try to allay or confirm suspicions they may have about school activities. If you are careful you can manipulate this situation so that it has a positive outcome. There is nothing like getting the leader of the school gate mafia up to her ears in glue and Plasticine on a regular basis to enable her to see how much work goes on in the school. Conversions of this sort are priceless; your greatest critic may rapidly become your closest ally.

Two simple tactics should make things easier. If you can, avoid putting parents into the same class as their children, and make it known that this is school policy. This helps parents to remain more objective about their activities, and also ensures that those who volunteer are more likely to be doing it for the right reasons. Secondly, be selective about the parents you use and the classes you place them in, at least until you are sure of your ground. You will find this a problem until you get to know everyone better, so a steady approach is advised.

Finally, here is a list — by no means exhaustive — of some of the activities in which parents or other volunteer helpers can be involved. The possibilities are almost limitless; in fact, the only limits are the time parents have available and the willingness of your staff to co-operate.

• Library activities — helping with changing books, advising on choice, covering and repairing books.
• Cutting up paper, covering books and making work-cards.
• Helping young children to change before and after PE.
• Hearing reading — particularly with good readers.
• Helping with art and craft activities in the classroom.

• Cleaning and washing equipment.
• Cooking.
• Accompanying staff and children on educational visits.
• Using special talents and skills with children.
• Talking to groups of children about their jobs, their past or their travels.

You may judge some of these activities to be inappropriate for your school, and there will certainly be others that you will wish to add. Try to vary the activities given to each parent, to avoid involving some parents always in menial tasks and others always in the more attractive activities. This will also enable you to build up a bank of expertise and experience.

You may find it useful to draw up a simple form for parents wishing to offer help, designed to find out what special skills or talents they have, and how you could make best use of their time in school. One example of such a form is shown below.

Parents' associations

Parents' associations in this country come in a number of forms, but most have the principal purpose of providing additional support and resources for the children's education. Fund raising, in all its many forms, has become the main activity in many associations.

Any headteacher would be well advised to study the constitution of the parents' association to see what its aims are, what it expects of the headteacher, and how much teacher involvement is anticipated. Remember when doing this that although the constitution is binding, it can be changed.

In any event, you are not obliged to accept the parents' association in its present form and, as a last resort, you are at liberty to disband and reform it on terms you find more acceptable.

A good relationship between the headteacher and the parents' association is vital to the association's success. The

Dear Parent,

You may know that, from time to time, parents are involved in work within the school — either helping directly in classrooms or assisting in other projects for the benefit of the children.

We are currently trying to draw up a list of parents who may be able to help in this way and, if you are interested, it would help us if you would answer the questions on the attached list and return it to us.

Thank you for your help,
Yours sincerely,

(Headteacher)

Name .... Child's class............

I am able to offer help regularly/occasionally (please delete where not applicable).

I am able to help on the following days of the week (please list)/any day of the week.

I would prefer to work in the morning/ afternoon/either morning or afternoon.

Please list any times or days when it would not be convenient for you to help.

I would rather work in classes/out of classes.

Please list overleaf any special interests or skills you have which might be useful to us.

relationship should be established early on and worked at until a mutually satisfactory conclusion is reached. There may sometimes be a conflict of aims and expectations, and you need to set ground rules and state the level of your own commitment. If, for example, you are not willing to attend every social function as a matter of course, this must be stated. Similarly, the headteacher's role on the committee or at general meetings has to be defined so that misunderstandings and embarrassments are avoided.

Fund raising by parents

The importance of parents' associations in the financial life of a typical primary school should not be underestimated. Headteachers have become more and more dependent upon fund raising for providing extra items of equipment in their schools.

This is not the place to make judgements on the wisdom or morality of such a course of action, except perhaps to comment on the irony of a situation which requires charitable donations of time and money in order to provide adequate modern equipment for the education of our young. Whatever we think, fund raising by parents is now a fact of life and the headteacher faces a few decisions when considering how best to manage the situation.

Usually parents' groups are well motivated to raise money, although it is generally much more helpful to them if they have a target to aim at. Ideally, fund raising should be associated with short-term achievable projects which have tangible results and which benefit large numbers of children. Parents understandably want to feel that their efforts are going to benefit their own children, and projects should be conceived with this in mind. It is far better to work to buy a new computer and associated equipment, which might take six months' or a year's fund raising, than to work for a swimming pool or library block which may take ten years and which may never benefit the children of the parents currently involved in the association.

The way in which projects are chosen and adopted is important because it says much about the relationship between the headteacher and the association. Although parents' groups may from time to time suggest ideas for spending their funds, it is generally preferable if proposals come from the school staff via the headteacher.

One method is to produce a 'shopping list' after staff consultation and submit this to the association for their agreement. The list should contain a range of items, possibly in order of priority, in various price brackets. Some may be fairly cheap and some very expensive, but all should have been chosen because they are both achievable and useful, while not belonging to the category of essentials which should be provided from public funds.

Submit the list either to the general meeting or to the committee, in accordance with accepted practice. Ask them to consider whether they would like to support any of the projects listed. This will give the meeting a chance to question the need for particular items and to draw up its own table of priorities, while allowing for the option of only adopting some of the projects. At the same time it ensures that anything which is paid for in this way is wanted by the school, and it offers one solution to the difficulties some headteachers experience when wanting to spend other people's money.

Parents usually welcome the chance for their funds to be used, and the association benefits from the continuity involved in buying some items at once and working towards others as long-term projects.

School brochure

All schools are required by law to publish certain information about themselves. The way in which this requirement is met varies from school to school, according to preference and to means, from a glossy professional brochure to a few sheets of hand-duplicated typescript.

The content matters more than the appearance. A glossy brochure containing badly-written, scant information is of little use to parents. Does the school booklet merely meet the law's requirements, or does it seek to answer parents' questions and to convey additional information?

The booklet should be reviewed regularly, and you should ensure that the amendments take account of the questions and issues raised by parents who have visited the school to discuss the admission of their children.

Although the content is of paramount importance, don't underestimate the power of good presentation in marketing the school. Try to produce your brochure in as professional a way as possible, and give thought to layout and design.

Check with the LEA to see if there is a typesetting service which you could use for your brochure. Those operating the service should be able to advise you about layout and illustrations, in order to help you achieve a professional result.

Failing this, use a word processor to produce the copy for your brochure. Check with teachers' centres to see if they have any facilities you could use.

Check-list for a school booklet

The following checklist covers some essential information for inclusion in any school booklet. The items which are required by statute to be included in the school's literature are indicated with an asterisk.

- *The school's name, address and telephone number, and its classification.
- *The name of the headteacher, deputy headteacher and chairperson of the board of governors.
- *The name and address of the local education authority.
- *School session times and term dates.
- *The school's admission policy; a statement of the criteria for admission, catchment area, target admission number, and any other relevant information.
- *The admission arrangements and procedure for appeals.
- A statement of the induction policy for new children.
- *A statement of the aims of the school.
- *Details of class and year group organisation.
- *A breakdown of the areas of the school's curriculum, including details of how the National Curriculum is being implemented in each year group.
- *An explanation of the mechanism for parents' complaints about the implementation of the National Curriculum.
- *General details about the time spent by each year group on each area of the curriculum.

- A statement about RE, and the arrangements for parents to withdraw their children if they wish.
- *A statement about the provision of sex education within the school.
- *The school's rules, and its stand on discipline. Explain pastoral arrangements and the methods for informing parents of disciplinary problems.
- *Details of school uniform, if any, with the approximate cost of each item.
- An explanation of the arrangements for parents to consult teachers about their children's progress.
- The school policy on educational visits.
- A statement about the place of the school within the community.
- A statement about any equal opportunities policies within the school.
- Any other information required by the LEA or the governors or generally deemed appropriate.

Some of the items listed above will change from year to year, so the information will have to be renewed annually. The booklet must contain a notification that the information included was correct at the time of publication.

Communicating with parents

Most schools these days have established systems for communication with parents. The school newsletter, appearing regularly or irregularly, weekly or termly, often manages to convey a whole range of information from changes in school rules to the successes of the netball team. Newsletters vary widely in style from school to school, and you could do worse than to look at some of the approaches adopted by colleagues before deciding on your own.

Headteachers who can maintain a chatty, friendly style in their newsletters, while managing to get the important messages across, are to be envied. Style, content and balance of material all play an important part in this process. The very nature of school newsletters means that their content will be varied. Beware of juxtaposing portentous messages about the National Curriculum and its impact on parents with requests for helpers at the forthcoming bring and buy sale. If you do, you may risk attaching the wrong degree of importance to one or both of the subjects!

One final point is that parents should be given as much notice as possible about future activities. As a parent I have suffered the problems associated with receiving notices about important school events two days before they are due, and this does nothing to improve the image of the school. Try to use a phased warning system. Send out a general list of dates for the events of the year or term as soon as these are known, then use a series of reminders, placing more importance on the items nearest in the calendar. The final stage in this process should be a letter of invitation to one particular event giving, in the case of parents' evenings, the specific times parents are invited to attend.

Some parents choose to judge schools and headteachers by the quality of their communication with the outside world. Whether you come to view parents as clients, customers, colleagues or partners, communication is a vital element in the relationship.

Chapter Eleven

Keeping a record

In search of a better system

Most primary schools have devised their own system for recording aspects of children's work and development. At the same time, in many schools, those who are responsible for completing the records are far from satisfied with what they are doing and are constantly seeking something better.

The quest for a better record-keeping system has preoccupied headteachers and their staffs for many years, since long before the advent of the National Curriculum. The intention of this chapter is to list some of the questions one should ask before setting about introducing a system. These questions may seem obvious, but asking them may help you to avoid some of the possible pitfalls.

Why keep records?
The first question to ask is, 'Why do we need to keep any records at all?' We cannot simply answer this by reference to the requirements of the National Curriculum, or by saying that schools have always kept records. Answers to the question must arise from within the school, from the staff themselves, and must relate to the ideas of continuity, professional achievement and

commitment. Above all, a system must have some measurable advantage for the children.

It is important to take into account the need to take an objective, long-term view of each child, in order to ensure that progress is being made and that any problems are picked up and dealt with promptly.

If you and your staff ask yourselves, 'Do we keep records because we want to, or because we have to?', the answer will say much about the way you view your role. Every aspect of record-keeping should be determined by need and by the aim of benefiting the children and improving their future education.

Answering the key question of why records are kept not only serves to determine levels of commitment, but also helps to define the form which records should take and the degree of detail they should contain.

What should we record?

Be clear about the information you want your records to contain. Do you intend to record information about pupils just in respect of the core subjects, or will other curriculum areas and other sorts of information be included? Do you intend to keep information about the children's physical development and their home and social circumstances?

It is useful to think in more detail about the range of material which can or should be recorded. Some areas which might be considered for inclusion are:

- Academic attainment in core subjects (progress through attainment targets),
- Academic attainment in other curriculum areas,
- Behaviour and attitudes,
- Physical development,
- Skills,
- Medical details,
- Social and external factors which might affect a child's work,
- Samples of work,
- Records of meetings with parents,
- Class teachers' reports,
- Information from previous schools.

Any record containing all this information in detail would be truly comprehensive, but it is also important to take care that records are kept short and readable.

The headteacher has to ensure that all aspects of record-keeping within the school can be justified educationally, that the records are manageable, that they have the support of the staff who are to implement them, and that they fulfil at least the minimum statutory requirements relating to pupil records. This has to be done within the constraints of time and cost. The headteacher has to account quite separately to the governors on the Annual Curriculum Return for the use of time and the balance of the curriculum, and to the parents and governors on various aspects of the National Curriculum; this may also make things difficult.

Teachers differ in opinion over the relevance and importance of record-keeping, so arriving at complete agreement about school records may prove difficult.

Who should see the records?

Who will normally have access to the children's records? For whom are the records primarily intended? Which members of staff are responsible for completing records, and who else will normally make an input?

You may well be able to reach agreement quite easily on the questions of access to records and responsibility for

completion, but guidelines and ground rules need to be established and agreed at an early stage in order to avoid misunderstandings and difficulties.

Records should be kept in a secure place, perhaps in a centrally-stored filing cabinet. Anybody who has genuine professional involvement with the child should have ready access to the files. Don't make it too difficult for teachers to gain access to the records; if two or three members of staff have a key to the cabinet, everyone should know who to approach whenever they want to look at the records.

Parents have a right to see their child's records, if they wish. It goes without saying that any information in the records should be written with the utmost discretion and tact, and should be capable of validation.

Who does the recording?

Most teachers probably accept that the principal responsibility for completion of records rests with class teachers. However, there are many other individuals and agencies who may be involved to a greater or lesser extent, depending on the content of the records. Support and special needs teachers, ancillaries, psychologists, parents, school nurses, 'the office'; all of these may have a role to play in the completion of individual children's records. The wisdom of including any or all of these people as a routine should be considered carefully at the planning stage.

Two factors must be taken into account. Firstly, there is the question of the relative value of the contributions. Schools need to be clear whether the contributors are likely to tell them anything they do not already know, and whether the information will ultimately benefit the children concerned. Secondly, there is the time factor. If so much time is spent approaching the various agencies for their contributions and discussing, reading and assessing the reports that valuable teaching time is lost, then the effort may be counter-productive.

Most teachers feel that children's records are of most use to future class teachers, and the material they want to include in records reflects this. Their input into a record takes account of the fact that it will be read by fellow teachers who will share common goals and ideals and who may have a shared understanding.

Will the records be used?

There is another factor related to this, which should be discussed among the staff at the planning stage of any record-keeping scheme. It is not uncommon for teachers to decline to refer to the records passed on by the previous teacher, at least for half a term or so, because of a wish not to prejudge the children. This action is frequently defended by comments such as, 'I like to make up my own mind about the children when they come up to me', or, 'I like to give them a fresh start and allow them to forget past mistakes.'

Although this is understandable in part, it is not a sound basis for a professional and integrated approach to education. The National Curriculum does not encourage such insularity, and continuity cannot be aided by such an attitude. If, in the course of a primary school career, a child works with seven teachers, all of whom share this view, continuity of learning is broken six times for periods of several months. This can be particularly damaging for children who may be experiencing learning or emotional difficulties.

This approach to record keeping implies a degree of mistrust of the views and experience of colleagues, which does little to support the notion of a team.

When do we have the time?

At some stage, agreement has to be reached about an acceptable work-load for teachers completing records on each child. There may be clear implications for directed time if the amount of work is large. It is important to seek agreement rather than to impose a system which may be difficult to manage, especially if the concept of relevance is not shared by the whole staff.

At what intervals will each record be completed or reviewed? Do you plan to update the records continuously, or at regular intervals? If you have a deadline for updating records it is easier to supervise, but once again mutual agreement on the method adopted is desirable.

When considering the timing of your record-keeping it is essential to keep in mind the work-load the system may impose on teachers, particularly those concerned with critical stages of assessment as determined by the National Curriculum. Too great a work-load may result in poorly-completed records and in the neglect of other tasks. If necessary, reach an agreement about other activities which may be sacrificed in order to make room for recording.

Ideally, any new system should either be absorbed into the existing one or should be an alternative to it. Otherwise there may be severe repercussions for time management and, in particular, for the allocation of directed time.

Whether the recording process is perceived as a continuous operation or as a routine activity carried out at regular, prescribed intervals, you will probably need to think about the possibility of some non-contact time for the teachers concerned. You must accept that the degree of commitment among the staff may vary considerably; any system should allow for this fact. At the same time it must be recognised that most teachers accept the need for recording and will enter into a programme willingly, provided that they see the requirements as relevant, manageable and professionally useful.

Remember, too, that compulsory record-keeping is effective only if it is accompanied by compulsory record-reading. Records are useless if no one ever looks at them, and this simple fact has been the downfall of many well-intentioned schemes.

How do we go about it?

How can you achieve a compromise between full and effective records which contain adequate information about the development, progress and learning of each child and the need for such records to be both simple to complete and easy to comprehend?

Can you introduce a system which will make it possible to ensure that a reasonable level of accuracy and consistency is maintained by each teacher involved in record-keeping? Getting it right requires a subtle blend of patience, experience, trial and error, agreement and understanding, which must be put together gradually.

Most teachers emphasise the importance of verbal interaction in their personal assessment and record-keeping, and no one should undervalue the importance of informal chats in the staffroom about particular children. Many teachers carry vast amounts of information about children around in their heads, much of which is never committed to paper. This represents a valuable resource available to the staff of any school. Tapping and channelling it is one of the functions of a record-keeping programme.

Deciding how the transfer of this and other information should take place is a significant part of the planning stage of the programme. Each teacher's informal knowledge may have to be committed to paper in the process of formal record-keeping, but success will depend on excluding irrelevant material and on establishing a manageable system for recording.

You may decide to devise a set of standard record sheets for various areas of development. If you have a member of staff responsible for record-keeping, he or she could lead a working party to draw up a sample sheet for each area. These sheets could then be produced and discussed at staff meetings.

Before implementing the record sheets, try them out, perhaps on an INSET day. Fill in some sheets amongst yourselves, then modify them in the light of any problems this activity reveals.

Once your system is in operation, try to review it annually.

Reviewing the existing system

The previous sections should have provided you with some starting points for coping with the problems associated with introducing a record-keeping system. Any system will be improved by the application of this question and answer technique. Most schools already have some method of record-keeping in operation, and usually the headteacher is faced with the task of organising and implementing a review and reform of the system. In some ways, this may be more difficult than starting from scratch.

You will need to question how and to what extent the present system falls short of the requirements that have arisen from the preceding questions. This will show which parts of the existing system must be adjusted and modified so as to meet more fully the targets set. There may be parts of the present system which are good and which should be retained.

The key to a record-keeping system

• All record-keeping should be seen as relevant to the role of a teacher by those required to complete the records.
• All information kept on record should have a justifiable value.
• Staff should agree a record-keeping policy collectively, as it is not possible to impose one satisfactorily.
• Records are only useful if they are structurally simple and if they are the result of a regular and systematic review.
• Teachers place great value on the process of verbal interaction. The spoken word plays an important part in the record-keeping and assessment process. The value of this contribution should not be overlooked in the building of a formal system.
• Teachers, like everyone else, want visual simplicity in records so that they can absorb the information easily.
• Compulsory record-keeping must be backed up by a requirement that records are read and acted upon. These are opposite sides of the same process, and it is altogether pointless to keep records unless they are read.
• A system of moderation must be designed to ensure that objectivity and credibility are maintained in the records.
• Clear guidelines should be drawn up stating who has access to records and who will normally make a contribution.
• It is important to recognise parents' rights of access to their child's records, particularly where the child's progress through the National Curriculum is concerned.

Chapter Twelve

Day-to-day concerns

Plenty has already been said about the need for a headteacher to develop co-operative management techniques, effective communication and good relationships with governors and the LEA. However, it is in the day-to-day running of the school that a headteacher's performance is most often judged. You may receive more complaints about trivialities than about what you consider to be serious matters; your judgement may be questioned more often on decisions concerning packed lunches than on major curriculum matters.

There are two ways of looking at this. The first is to feel quite pleased. If parents only complain about trivial things, it must mean that they have no problem with the serious issues. The alternative is to take the parents' point of view. Most people feel happier dealing with matters they can identify with, and about which they feel confident. Concern about minor matters may hide a deeper worry which parents might feel unable to articulate. Complaints about trivial matters may be symptoms of concern about the way a school is being run, and should not be ignored.

The headteacher's performance is likely to be judged – by the 'customers' at least – on a day-to-day basis. This may influence some of his or her particular actions and decisions. However, it is necessary to retain some perspective and not to be unduly influenced by the short-term viewpoint. It is worth remembering that the loudest voices do not necessarily belong to the majority.

This chapter aims to examine some of the more common features of the day-to-day running of a school, to look at alternative approaches and to suggest ways of avoiding some of the common pitfalls. As always, a broad view is presented from which you can choose an approach which best suits your school and circumstances. This chapter will also examine in a broader context the concept of the management of change as it relates to the role of the headteacher in a primary school.

An unusual feature of headship is that so many things are taken for granted both by colleagues and by parents. So much knowledge and wisdom is expected of you by those you deal with. So many practices in school occur without question because they have always done so. So many traditions – both within schools and in the world of education at large – seem unquestioned and unquestionable.

As headteacher, you have to introduce your own outlook and philosophies into your school, and in doing so you will need to walk the tightrope between conservatism and radicalism. Too much change and you are labelled revolutionary, too little and you will be seen to be ineffectual.

Remember that, given the constraints of the building and the restrictions on staffing and budget, there is little that cannot be changed if you consider it valuable to the development of the school. To give some useful examples of changes that can be made fairly easily, four typical areas of organisation will be examined.

The school day

The length of a school day is rather like that of the proverbial piece of string. Some authorities have laid down guidelines and rulings for the schools under their jurisdiction, and some have not. Where there are no guidelines, what occurs in schools is usually a blend of tradition, good sense and mythology. You would do well to look closely at the arrangements in existence, to see if they are the best way of serving children, staff and community.

If you wish to change the length of the school day, or indeed to make any variations to the times of sessions, you will need the approval of the governors. In practice this is usually not too difficult, as long as you have sound reasons for your request and your proposals are not too extreme. Assuming that approval will probably be forthcoming from the governors – at least eventually – let's examine the sorts of changes which may be possible.

We can start by looking at the legal background. Before directed time, there were no conditions of service relating to teachers' hours or school sessions except the general statement in Section 23 of the 1944 Act (now repealed), the Schools Amending Regulations 1966, and the Educational Regulations 1981. These specified at least three hours of secular instruction each day for pupils under eight, and at least four hours for classes in which the children were mainly eight and over. Additionally, it was required that the day should be divided into two sessions.

These specifications may have given rise to the practice in many schools of having a shorter working day for infants than for juniors. This may sometimes have been thought desirable, but it was certainly not required by law, and it often gave rise to administrative headaches and problems of supervision when half of the school regularly finished before the other half.

Custom and practice therefore seem to have determined the length of the school day, and the morning and afternoon breaks have traditionally been considered teaching time. The 1987 Teachers' Conditions of Service Act re-stated the teachers' right to a lunch break, but said nothing about other breaks. DES Circular 14/89, however, seems to have established that teaching time now *excludes* registration periods, breaks and collective worship, although these must presumably still be included in directed time.

Since the Education Reform Act 1988, governors have been responsible for determining the session times in their schools. Some guidelines in the form of minimum lengths for the school week were given in DES Circular 14/89 and, more recently, in Circular 7/90. The intention is clearly to work towards an acceptable minimum, and working weeks of 21 hours for children between five and seven, and 23 hours for children between eight and thirteen are proposed. These guidelines specifically exclude break, registration and collective worship, and it seems likely that some schools will eventually find it necessary to lengthen their working day.

The length of the lunch break is something else that should be looked at carefully. Probably the main controlling factor here is the need to accommodate all the children in the dining hall. This may require a number of sittings. However, you must balance this against the problems which arise in the course of a long lunch break, particularly on a wet day. You should keep the lunch break as short as possible, even if this means having a staggered break. Although teachers have a contractual entitlement to a lunch break, no length is specified other than that it should be 'reasonable'.

One clear advantage of a short lunch break is the possibility of an earlier finish in the afternoon. This is important because of the number of meetings and after-school activities which teachers are now obliged to attend. An earlier finish to afternoon school gives greater scope for after-school activities for the children as well. It may enable them to participate in school clubs and activities, while still ensuring that they get home before dark in the winter.

The message is that your arrangements and session times should reflect the needs of your school and the community it serves; they should not simply be dictated by tradition or by decree from outside. If you are convinced that what you are proposing is right, you should find no difficulty in gaining support from governors, staff and parents, providing that the DES regulations about the minimum length of the teaching week are observed.

Arrangement of classes

If your school has a standard one, two or three forms of entry, and if you are fortunate enough to be able to admit a constant number of children each year, then most of this section will not apply to you. If, on the other hand, you have half or other fractions of a form of entry and uneven intakes from year to year, you may wish to look at alternative ways of organising your school to make the best use of resources.

Conventional age groups

The traditional arrangement for organising classes in primary schools is, of course, to assume that the number of children can be divided neatly into thirty, or thirty-five, or whatever the acceptable class size is, and to arrange the classes into chronological age groups.

In a conventionally-grouped class, the maximum age difference between the oldest and the youngest child is twelve months. The cut-off date means that some children can be as little as one day older or younger than children in the next age group, and may suffer from permanently being the oldest or the youngest in the class. This fact, added to the problems associated with the variations in admissions arrangements across the country, shows how children can be disadvantaged by the rigidity of the system.

In some authorities children are admitted at the beginning of the school year in which they are five; in others they may not be admitted until the term in which they are five. Despite these variations, they all leave primary school at the end of the summer term of the school year in which they are eleven. How much better if all children were obliged to spend a fixed number of terms in primary school before transferring, and how useful this consistency would be, given the requirements of the National Curriculum and assessment at fixed ages.

Changing the arrangements

How can you compensate for uneven year groups, for half-forms of entry, for children who are permanently the 'babies' of the class? One way is to rearrange the classes so as to reduce the effect of these factors. This is not always an ideal solution, but it is an approach which may work in some situations.

To carry out this type of rearrangement you need, to begin with, two facts: the number of classes you wish to operate, and the school roll. Simple division then gives you the class size, and you can allocate children to classes starting with the oldest and working downwards. If, for example, you have a roll of 310 and ten classrooms, each class will contain 31 children arranged strictly in order of age.

Advantages and disadvantages

This system has drawbacks, but it also has great advantages. The biggest disadvantage is the attitude of some teachers and many parents to this type of arrangement. Most will insist on seeing the classes as 'mixed', and will fail to see how, for instance, third years and second years can be taught together. If the children are considered as individuals, and work individually or in small groups, this is not a problem, for even a conventionally-grouped class contains a wide range of ability and work rates. If, on the other hand, the children are taught as a whole class, then so called 'mixed age groups' can be harmful. Arguably, however, the disadvantages are only marginally greater than in a conventional class taught by the same approach.

One of the most common objections to this way of working is based on the notion that the children are of different ages. But the variation in ages may well be no greater than in a class formed according to traditional age groups; young third years may be very close in age to old second years. You may even find that the difference in age between the oldest and youngest in a class will be reduced if this form of non-traditional grouping is used. In fact, the bigger the school, the smaller the gap is likely to be.

From an administrative viewpoint, this method of class organisation has many advantages. It makes the distribution of children among the classes very straightforward, and allows forward planning based on a knowledge of the exact class sizes. In some respects, because of the reduced age difference, the teachers' jobs can be made easier, providing they adopt an individual or group orientated approach and don't try to teach the whole class.

Other systems

There are other ways of organising the structure of classes, and these should not be overlooked when deciding on the most appropriate method for your school. The more conventional form of 'vertical grouping', which deliberately sets out to mix traditional age groups by combining two, three or four consecutive age groups has been widely criticised for making the teacher's job difficult, although it may offer some advantages as a method of organisation in certain circumstances.

Many headteachers go to great lengths not to mix infant children with junior children, even to the extent of tolerating an oversize class on one side or another of the 'Great Divide'. This aversion to mixing the two stages may have more to do with traditional practice and a desire to maintain the distinct identities of two internal departments than with developmental theory or educational philosophy.

Whatever system you decide to adopt in your school, you should be satisfied that you have looked at all the available options. Your decision should be based on suitability and practicality rather than on a wish to uphold tradition or to avoid antagonism and objections from staff and parents.

Some examples of different class arrangements are shown overleaf to help you consider the possible alternatives.

As always, if you plan to make changes, first be sure that you can justify them educationally and administratively and then push ahead. If you appear to be unsure or uncertain you will find little support from your colleagues or from the parents, and change is likely to prove difficult. If you are confident, however, and the rationale for your proposed changes is sound, doing what you want to do may turn out to be less difficult than you had thought.

Sample class arrangements

One form entry

Marshland Primary:
Classrooms - 7
Staff - 7 full-time plus headteacher
Roll - 180 made up of:
reception - 30
primary 1 - 28
primary 2 - 28
primary 3 - 25
primary 4 - 23
primary 5 - 20
primary 6 - 26

Option 1: Traditional
This would give you seven classes based on the traditional age groups. The classes would be of various sizes, with one teacher per class. The disadvantages are that class sizes are unequal, all available teachers are used, and there is a twelve-month span of age between the youngest and oldest children in each class.

Option 2: Age-ordering
This option results in six age-ordered classes of 30, with one teacher per class, and one spare teacher for classroom support and other roles. The only obvious disadvantage is that it disturbs the traditional age cut-off point of 31 August. The advantages are that it balances the numbers of children within the classes, and releases one teacher from full-time class responsibility. You may also find that there is less than a twelve-month gap in age between the oldest and youngest children in any class.

Option 3: Partial vertical grouping
Primary 5 and 6 could be combined, and then split into two classes in equal proportion. Primary 3 and 4 could be combined and split in the same way, as could Primary 1 and 2. Reception would be left undisturbed. This would give classes of 30, 28, 28, 24, 24, 23, 23. There would be little advantage in this approach with this distribution of numbers, especially as the age span in any one class could be as much as two years.

One and a half form entry

Egon Ronay Primary:
Classrooms - 11
Staff - 11 full-time plus headteacher
Roll - 301 made up of:
reception - 50
year 1 - 45
year 2 - 42
year 3 - 43
year 4 - 41
year 5 - 40
year 6 - 40

Option 1: Traditional
Traditional grouping would not be possible unless classes of 40 children or more are acceptable.

Option 2: Age-ordering
By arranging classes in strict age-order, you can arrive at ten classes of 30, using ten teachers and releasing a spare for support. The gap in age between the oldest and the youngest child in each class may well be considerably less than twelve months.

If you wished to use all eleven teachers and classrooms you could consider splitting the 50 reception children into groups of 25 and having nine remaining classes arranged in age order. These classes would each contain 27 or 28 children.

Option 3: Partial vertical grouping
If you tried this, you would find it necessary to mix the year groups in different combinations. The 80 children in Primary 5 and 6 could be divided between two classes of 30 and the remaining 20 — presumably the youngest — could be recombined with Primary 4 to give two classes of 30, and so on. It gets rather complex and the advantages of Option 2 become clearer.

Two form entry
Brick Street Primary
Classrooms - 14
Staff - 14.3 plus headteacher
Roll - 399 made up of:
reception - 60
primary 1 - 53
primary 2 - 56
primary 3 - 60
primary 4 - 58
primary 5 - 53
primary 6 - 59

Option 1: Traditional
This is probably the most practical option, given the reasonable balance of year groups.

Option 2: Age-ordering
If you separate the reception classes into two groups of 30 and then consider the remainder in terms of age-ordering you could reduce your number of classes to 13. This would increase class sizes to 32, but it would save a teacher for support work.

Option 3: Partial vertical grouping
You could try this in a limited form where there are not enough children in any one year group to fill two complete forms. This would also enable you to release a teacher for support work within the school.

Staffing arrangements

The teachers you work with are primary teachers and should be able and qualified to work with any age group within the school. Some will have favourite age groups, and some will also have areas in which they are particularly able or in which they experience difficulties. By and large, however, these variations in attitudes or abilities have more to do with relative experience than with innate characteristics.

Many headteachers now recognise the benefits of staff mobility within the school and try to foster an atmosphere in which teachers welcome a change of classroom or year group on a regular basis. The days when the only male teacher always took the fourth year juniors or when the infants' and juniors' staff formed two distinct cohorts within the school have now largely passed, as teachers have come to recognise the value of shared experience and breadth of knowledge within a school. It is important to cultivate the idea of a whole-school approach to learning and the curriculum.

When planning year groups and teacher allocation, you must balance your own personal philosophy with the needs of the school. It is important to consider the past experience of the teachers concerned and to decide whether it is best to use this immediately in respect of a class, or whether to use it as a foundation for developing new experiences of teaching in new contexts. Initially this broadening process is mainly for the benefit of the teacher, but ultimately the school as a whole will also benefit.

If you have a policy of changing teachers and year groups regularly, you have to be careful that a particular class does not come into contact with the same teacher too frequently. One of the advantages of the class teaching system is the variety of personalities and teaching styles with which a child normally comes into contact in the course of seven years. The weaknesses of a particular teacher in one area may be offset by the strengths of another, with the result that at the end of the primary phase children should have a well-rounded experience. The realities of the situation may not be quite so rosy, but too much exposure to the same teacher is to be avoided, whether the teacher is good or bad.

The headteacher who wishes to make staffing changes against the custom of the school may come up against opposition. In this situation you must be positive about the benefits to teachers and children, know the personalities involved, and be prepared to point to examples of successful practice elsewhere. As a general rule it is wise to avoid extremes. The reception teacher who finds that next year she is to have fourth year juniors may have difficulty in accepting the idea, whereas a gradual move over a few years may be more acceptable.

Parents often have quaint notions about the pecking order in schools. Many believe that a teacher who is moved from top infants to reception has been demoted. This view of the hierarchy of schools is also shared by some teachers.

If headteachers develop a policy of staff mobility and parents and staff see that it is multi-directional, and not just a case of 'promotion' from the lower classes to the top ones, the old-fashioned attitudes should disappear. With luck, they will be replaced by an understanding of the interdependence of staff within a primary school, and the need to broaden the experience of everyone within the school.

Directed time

When the concept of directed time was imposed on teachers in 1987, headteachers found that one problem had been solved, only to be replaced by another. Teachers no longer had to attend their many meetings and out-of-school activities on a strictly voluntary basis, but headteachers now had the problem of managing a finite working week.

In many primary schools, directed time has had a minimal effect. Teachers who always gave their time willingly without watching the clock have, in general, continued to do so, while those who always knew exactly what could or could not be asked of them have continued to present a management problem.

You will have to decide whether to impose a rigid structure on the staff, detailing exactly how the 1,265 directed hours of the school year are to be worked, or whether to leave it more open and rely on old-fashioned professional commitment. It is not an easy choice.

In many ways the first of these options seems the most effective. Everyone knows where they stand, what they are required to do and the exact extent of their commitments. The headteacher knows what calls he or she can make on the staff and can plan a management approach accordingly.

There are, however, drawbacks. Using a rigid approach, you risk alienating those of your staff who have previously worked well and conscientiously undirected. If you impose a formal starting time of 8.30am, you may upset those teachers who regularly arrive at 8am. This is a slight risk, perhaps, but one which is worthy of consideration.

If your approach is rigid you risk excluding the possibility of flexibility – a key feature of school management. You will be less able to make occasional extra demands on your staff in one respect in return for concessions in other areas. This process of give and take was a common feature of pre-1987 staff management, and had much to commend it. Schools which do not acknowledge this need for flexibility and which operate a management system without this element of humanity are not pleasant places in which to work.

The third disadvantage of this approach is that it tends to turn the headteacher into a supervisor instead of a team-member who shares management responsibility with the staff while at the same time exercising a leadership function. The injudicious use of directed time not only appears to increase the power of the headteacher over the staff, but also weakens the professional role of the staff in the school structure. Any move which broadens the gap between headteacher and staff in this way should be avoided.

The alternative of taking a more liberal approach to staff management needs very careful handling. Like any liberal approach, it is open to abuse by the unscrupulous. Before adopting either approach, you must know the people you are working with and weigh up the possible gains and losses. Adopting a freer interpretation of directed time leaves you with the opportunity, should things go wrong, of imposing firmer control.

Whichever approach is taken, it is essential that you should be well aware of what is possible within the scope of directed time. This requires a degree of understanding of the law relating to teachers' conditions of service.

Headteachers may require their teachers to be available for work on no more than 195 days in a year, and during these days teachers can only be required to be available for a total of 1,265 hours. This means, quite simply, that directed time cannot take place outside the 195 days of school year and that if you choose to direct staff to work on Saturdays or during school holidays, these days must be deducted from the total of 195.

The implications of this for school journeys and sports fixtures were recognised early on as being quite serious. It is important, therefore, for you to be quite clear, and to make sure that staff are equally clear, about the distinction between time which is directed and time which is voluntary. If confusions arise they can lead to severe management difficulties, especially in a rigidly defined structure.

The second important condition which has to be noted is the staff entitlement to a break at midday. Although the length of such a break is not stipulated, it has to exist and, consequently, you are unable to direct time for more than a fraction of the school lunch break. The teachers' break does not have to correspond exactly with the school break, and there is some room for manoeuvre in this respect. Directed meetings and other activities at lunchtimes can be fraught with difficulties, however, and it is advisable to look for alternatives if staff are not prepared to attend voluntarily.

A good tactic to adopt when considering directed time is to list all the activities staff might normally be required to participate in during the course of a year, and to total the amount of hours involved. If these figures are made available to staff, without necessarily any suggestion that directed time is being invoked, they may come to an understanding about what is required of them. If they recognise that their normal commitment is within the 1,265 hours, there should be no problem with having to direct hours. The key point to remember is that working practices which result from negotiation are likely to be far more productive than those which result from imposition.

A typical year might be divided thus:

Teaching day 9am to 12 midday and 1.15pm to 3.30pm, 190 days per year:

5 ¼ hours X 190	= 997 ½ hours
5 INSET days @ 5 ½ hours	= 27 ½ hours
4 parents' meetings @ 4 hours	= 16 hours
20 staff meetings @ 1 hour	= 20 hours
2 concerts @ 2 hours	= 4 hours
¼ hour before and after school X 190	= 95 hours
TOTAL:	**1160 hours**

This arrangement, which is a very general example but which provides for many of the typical requirements in the primary school programme, still leaves over 100 hours uncommitted. Such a plan of time, interpreted fairly liberally, may be useful in schools in which teacher attendance has been stipulated for set periods after school without any associated reason. This sort of regime was widespread in the early days of directed time.

To use directed time to require staff to attend a staff meeting lasting, say, one hour a week seems reasonable. To use it to require staff to remain behind in school for a fixed period each day or week with no duty specified might seem churlish, and it may not be a good way of improving morale or getting any more work done. It may seem rather extreme to say that a headteacher who needs to invoke directed time in order to motivate his staff is demonstrating a breakdown in communication and leadership, but there may be some truth in this point of view.

Managing change

These examples have shown how aspects of a school's organisation can be based on firm philosophies, and how changes, even quite small ones, can have far-reaching outcomes. It is also worth noting the extent to which a headteacher's interpretation of his or her role and responsibilities can influence the success of policies for change.

In what must be the soundest and most memorable piece of advice I ever recall receiving in my early days of headship, a Local Authority adviser said to me that I should not be in too much of a hurry to change everything in my new school, no matter how appalling or frustrating I found it. He reminded me, however, that it is possible to get away with almost anything in education as long as you don't refer to it as change.

'Call it change', he said, 'and they will be round your ears like a pack of wolves baying for your resignation. Call it a development or even a review and they will probably welcome it and offer you every support.'

In order to be successful at managing change, you must be certain that the changes you envisage are valid and justified. If *you* are not convinced, you have no hope of convincing others. You must also be aware of the sources of possible opposition and support, both within the school and outside.

In many respects staff are both the most important and the most difficult people to influence. You must be aware that their opposition may not be overt, and that the latent type is often worse. Teachers may pay lip-service to an idea, and then just carry on as before. This can present difficulties which far outweigh those associated with outright hostility.

It is also essential to have a manageable time-scale. Many initiatives for change have failed because too short a time has been allowed for them.

A headteacher should be someone who questions everything — every action, every practice, every arrangement — and who works towards a scheme of school organisation based on the school itself and the children and the community it serves, not on the perceptions, prejudices or ignorance of others. There is a paramount need to question every motive and, where there is an indication of misinformation or a lack of educational value, to work for change and reform.

The headteacher should be a prime mover, the principal architect of change in the school he or she serves. Managing change is a difficult activity and requires a degree of skill and experience which many of us find hard to muster, but it is essential in modern primary education that the headteacher should succeed both in the effective management of change and in taking all the staff along as well.

Contents

	Acknowledgements	4
	About the Photographer	4
	Introduction	5
One	Royal Three Counties Show, Friday 17–Sunday 19 June	7
Two	The Cotswold Show and Food Festival, Saturday 2–Sunday 3 July	32
Three	Tewkesbury Classic Vehicle Festival, Sunday 21 August	51
Four	Winchcombe Country Show, Monday 29 August	66
Five	Moreton in Marsh Show, Saturday 3 September	82
Six	Frampton Country Fair, Sunday 11 September	99
Seven	Cotswold Living Landscape Festival, Sunday 18 September	113

Acknowledgements

Thank you to all the show organisers from each event and to my friends and family, who have helped and supported me throughout this project.

About the Photographer

Hollie Crawshaw is a rural photographer based in the Forest of Dean in Gloucestershire, South West England. After studying for a degree in Editorial and Advertising Photography, Hollie specialised in capturing stories based on the British countryside, agriculture and rural life. Hollie is passionate about her subject matter and has a keen interest in animals. Her photographic approach is recognised for its truthful appeal and documentary style.

Introduction

Gloucestershire, in the South West of England, is home to numerous country shows, showcasing the very best of British farming, food and crafts. Usually held in the summer months, among the beautiful regional landscapes, these shows celebrate rural life and have a vast historical importance in keeping alive some of the oldest traditions. Most of Gloucestershire's shows have been running for many years and attract thousands of people each time. Many visitors return annually and generations of families, especially those in the farming communities, consider shows as a major event within their industry and social calendars. Attractions vary from show to show but many include livestock, countryside demonstrations, rallies, market stalls and competitions, with spectators of all ages enjoying these summer days out.

This book documents seven country shows held across Gloucestershire during the 2016 show season. These include the 31st Frampton Country Fair, the first ever Living Landscape Festival organised by the Cotswold Conservation Board and the famous Royal Three Counties, attended by the Princess Royal and BBC *Countryfile* presenter Adam Henson. By demonstrating the relationships between people, land and animals, the photos convey a true sense of community, unity and social interaction. The series aims to reference the early black-and-white images of old shows, highlighting the traditional values and timeless quality of these events. By picking out the finer details as well as the main aspects, the images capture exactly what it is like to be at the shows in an honest and observational way.

Most show days start with early morning planning, where farmers wash, dry, groom and spray their livestock in preparation for a day of competition. Traders set up their stalls filled with home-made food, produce, gifts and services, and entertainers ensure their acts are ready for the main arena performance in front of hundreds of onlookers.

Once the gates are open, the showground fills with excited families picking up show guides, looking at site maps and pointing out which events they don't want to miss. As the day goes on farmers, growers and creators are rewarded for their hard work and win prizes within their classes. Children enjoy the fun of the fair, interacting with animals and watching grand arena entertainment. Many spectators experience the array of fresh food available and shop among the rows of marquees, stalls and retail pavilions. The excitement and anticipation felt at these shows is instantly recognisable when looking through the images in this book. The photographs capture the atmosphere, attitudes and spirit of all those who attend and applaud rural life, striving to preserve this important aspect of British heritage.

One

Royal Three Counties Show, Friday 17–Sunday 19 June

Held at the renowned Three Counties Showground and attended by HRH Princess Anne, the annual Royal Three Counties Show celebrates the Herefordshire, Gloucestershire and Worcestershire countryside over three full days. The show is dedicated to the promotion of agriculture and is one of the biggest livestock shows in the country.

The 2016 show attracted 90,000 people, who enjoyed main arena attractions including the King's Troop Royal Horse Artillery, a Grand Parade of Livestock, and the Parachute Regiment Freefall Display Team – the Red Devils. The National Federation of Young Farmers took part in competitions – sheep shearing, showjumping, food, drink, and animals were all judged. Exhibitors travelled from far and wide hoping to win first-place red rosettes in significant industry society shows. These national breeds included the British Blonde, Longhorn, Dexter and British White Cattle as well as the Beltex and Hebridean sheep. Others included the Portland Sheep Breeders Premier Show and the RASE Cup, which for the first time in its history saw regional Gloucester cattle win the dairy and dual-purpose Burke Trophy. The Royal Three Counties boasts numerous arenas and various designated villages including a sport, equine, military and farming village. The location of this show is particularly picturesque, sitting under the famous Malvern Hills.

A farming family showing their sheep in the ring.

The judge analyses each animal in the show ring.

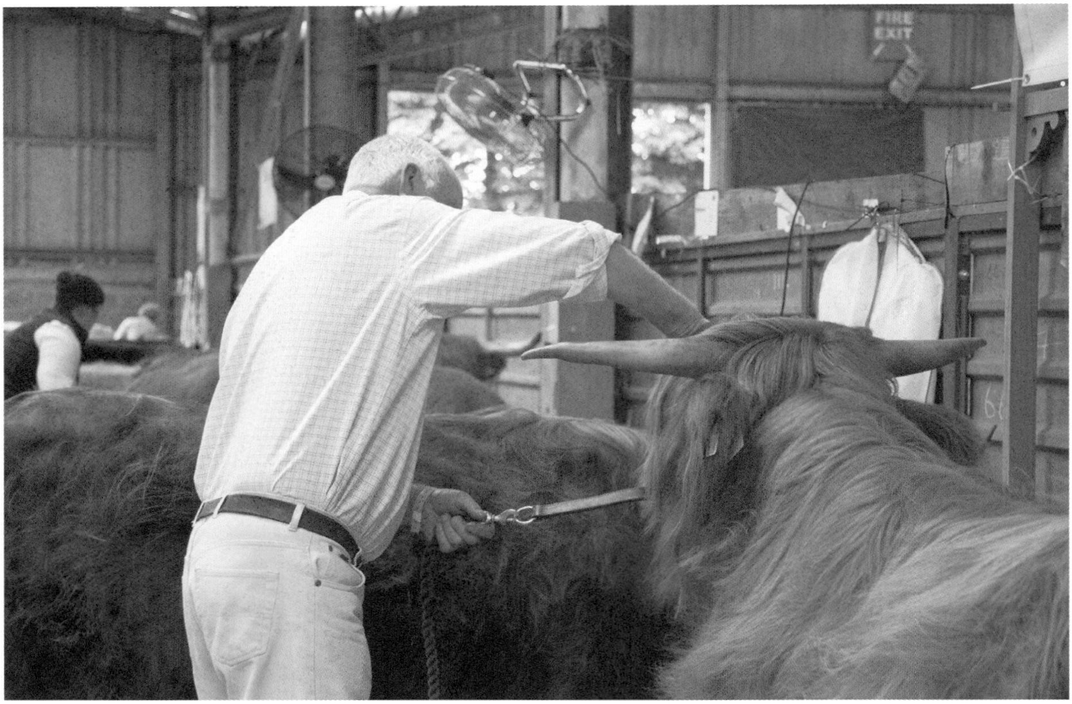

A farmer combs his cattle for the competitive Highland class.

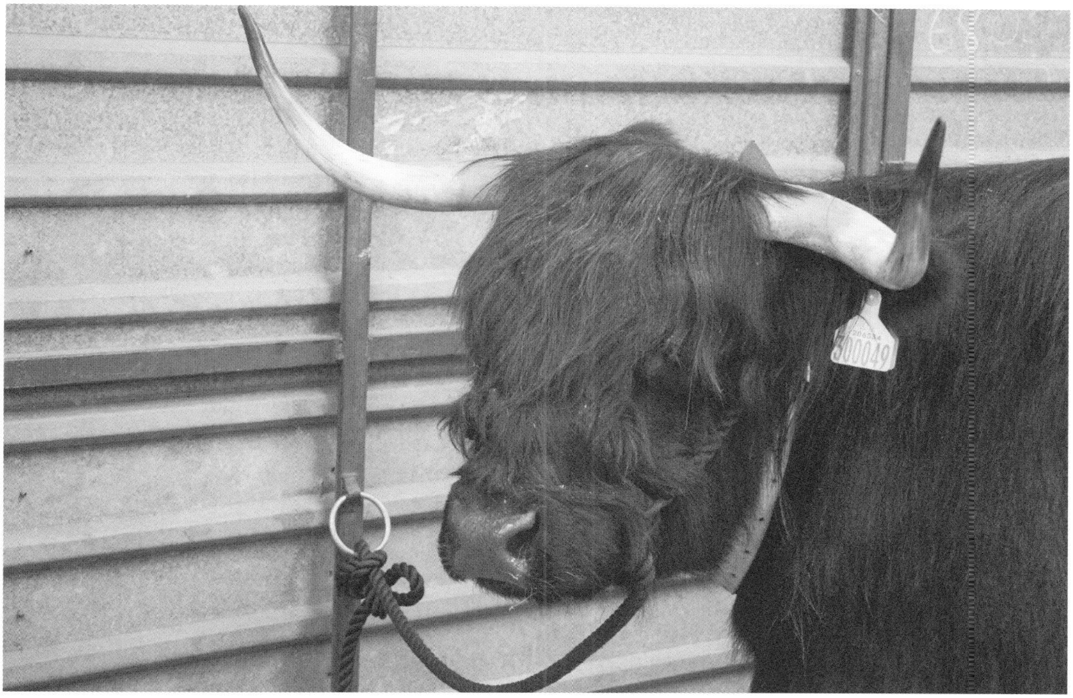

A cow stays in the cattle shed waiting to be groomed.

A horse and its owners enjoy the equine events of the day.

Participant waits on the sidelines for her turn to compete in the competition.

Vintage vehicles on show.

Girl looks around the cages of competing poultry.

Vintage tractor.

Goat inside one of the white show tents.

Visitors enjoy tasting the local honey on sale.

First, second and third prize hives.

An honesty jar left to take money for recipes.

Exhibits in the bees and honey section.

Horse owners apply Show White Powder to their horse's feathers.

Eggs are displayed for viewing, showing an array of colours, shapes and sizes.

Judges examine the chickens for prize-giving.

Winner of first place.

The eggs are judged in their various classes.

Wall of poultry entered in the bird classes.

The King's Troop Royal Horse Artillery in the Main Arena.

Mounted soldiers of The King's Troop Royal Horse Artillery.

Competitors enjoy the rivalry of shearing sheep.

Crowds gather beneath the famous Malvern Hills.

Farmer competes in the sheep-shearing race.

Livestock owner washes her cattle in preparation.

Cattle are kept in stores before being led into the rings.

Show calf.

A farmer displays the certificates and rosettes they have achieved.

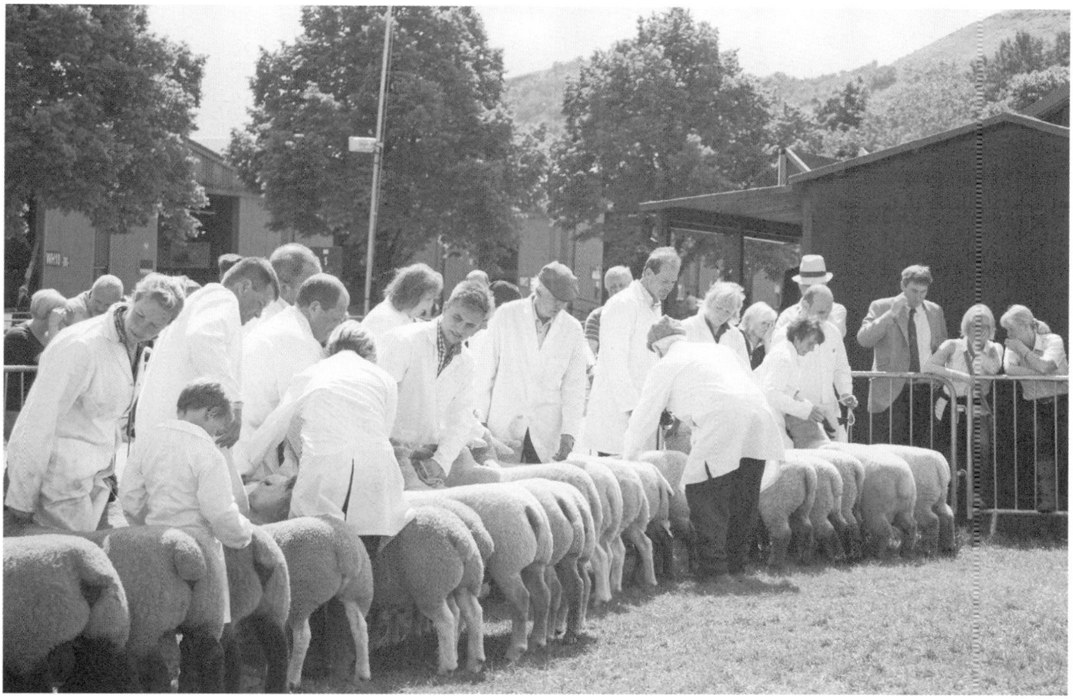

Sheep breeders show their sheep in formation for the judge to view.

Inside the cattle shed.

A judge and competitor taking part in the Grand Parade.

Royal Patron Princess Anne enters the members' tent with presidents and sponsors.

Winner shows his prizeworthy cattle in the Livestock Parade.

A farmer exhibits his award-winning cow.

A Highland cow is showed around the ring on a halter.

Grand Arena commentator explains each animal breed to the audience.

Members enjoy the Grand Arena entertainment.

Sheep winner enters the Main Arena for the annual Grand Parade of Livestock.

Young competitors show off their animals.

Brass band procession, part of The King's Troop Royal Horse Artillery.

Two

The Cotswold Show and Food Festival, Saturday 2–Sunday 3 July

Spread across 100 acres and organised by Lord Bathurst, this show was highly commended in Visit England's 2015 Awards for Excellence. Since its first show in September 1989, the Cotswold Show and Food Festival has run every year. However, in 2001, along with the rest of the UK, Gloucestershire was struck by the devastating foot-and-mouth outbreak. Moving livestock was banned and inevitably Lord Bathurst had to cancel the Cotswold Show, which returned in 2002.

The event continues to grow year upon year and is held in the historical grounds and gardens of Cirencester Park, a Grade II-listed country house. Thousands of people descend on the show to enjoy shopping, family entertainment and country pursuits. The 2016 show saw the Royal Signals Motorcycle Display Team, Shetland Pony Grand National, dog displays, clay pigeon shooting, and falconry. Animals are a large attraction and the Rare Breed Survival Trust had its own marquee containing livestock to see, pet, feed and interact with. Over eighty different pure-breed birds were also on show and specialists gave advice on equine, beekeeping, and fishing. The show has a special connection with food and the Food Hall featured seventy top producers selling and promoting their fresh quality cheese, bread, meats, relishes and cakes. The Cookery Theatre held engaging demonstrations by award-winning chefs, and stalls served delicious hot food, afternoon tea and alcoholic favourites!

Recently clipped sheep.

Handmade walking sticks.

Showshopper looks through box of garden dibbers.

Selection of walking sticks for sale.

Meerkats draw in the show visitors.

Vintage Nuffield Tractor.

Impressive bird on display in the falconry area.

A traditional spinning wheel in use.

Inside the Rare Breed Survival Trust tent.

Vintage working engine.

Woman attends to the chickens in the poultry tent.

Woodcarver demonstrates his rural craft.

Lady rides side-saddle, dressed in costume.

A traditional shepherd's hut on display to explore.

Historic farming equipment and tools for sale.

Themed weathervane.

Garden plants and flower stall.

Timber hauliers give woodcutting demonstrations.

A fine art foundry worker displays his casting skills.

Groups of friends and families watch arena amusements.

Retail stalls sell countryside fashion.

Farming-themed family entertainment.

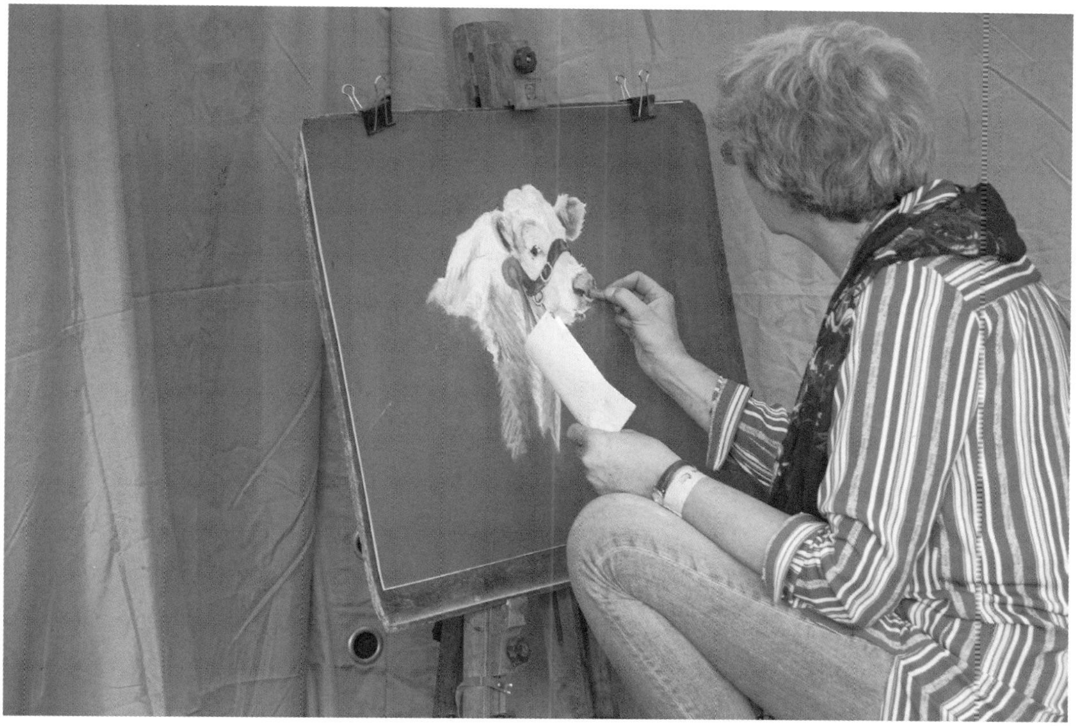

An artist draws from a show photograph.

Motorcyclists display outstanding balancing tricks.

The Royal Signals Motorcycle Display Team captivate their audience with an impressive formation.

Collection of dog collars.

Bystanders enjoy seeing the work of a horse specialist and learn practical horsemanship skills.

A traditional Hereford steer welcomes visitors into the RBST tent.

One of the many different breeds of birds at the show.

Sheep fleeces from the Cotswold sheep breed.

Onlookers watch The Royal Signals Motorcycle Display Team perform stunts using fire.

Bunting being used to decorate a white show tent.

A dog trainer performs professional canine routines.

The RBST tent containing various animal breeds.

Three

Tewkesbury Classic Vehicle Festival, Sunday 21 August

In its sixth year, the Tewkesbury Classic Vehicle Festival exhibited over 700 classic vehicles including cars, motorcycles, vans and the odd vintage tractor. The impressive show is a charitable event organised by the Tewkesbury Rotary Club and showcases cars spanning more than 100 years of history. Strolling through the numerous rows of vehicles, victors can expect to be taken back through time, listening to live music from past eras and seeing retro costumes. The total monetary worth of all the cars at the event is in its millions, with treasured Ferraris and valuable Rolls-Royces making up some of the luxurious brands. Trade stands and market stalls sell valuable collectables as well as mechanical parts, old equipment and memorabilia. The live period music was performed by the Haywood Sisters and people from all over the country came to enjoy a British- and American-themed carnival atmosphere.

The one-day festival was held on the 54 acres of Tewkesbury School playing fields and raised money for both the Rotary Club and the Midlands Air Ambulance. The location is just 200 yards away from the motorway, with easy access from Junction 9 off the M5.

Spectacular line-up of historic motors.

A selection of retro car signs.

Classic silver horns.

A stall sells second-hand vehicle parts and memorabilia.

Caps for sale.

Various oil cans.

Collectable tractor mugs.

Car owners clean and polish their precious motors.

A Riley classic car grill.

Front details of a Riley.

Visitors explore the impressive selection of motorbikes at the show.

The famous Spirit of Ecstasy on a Rolls-Royce bonnet.

Exhibitors pack show necessities into the back of their vintage car.

Car owner relaxes by his valuable asset.

Men have a conversation sat in the back of their pickup trucks.

An old Austin car.

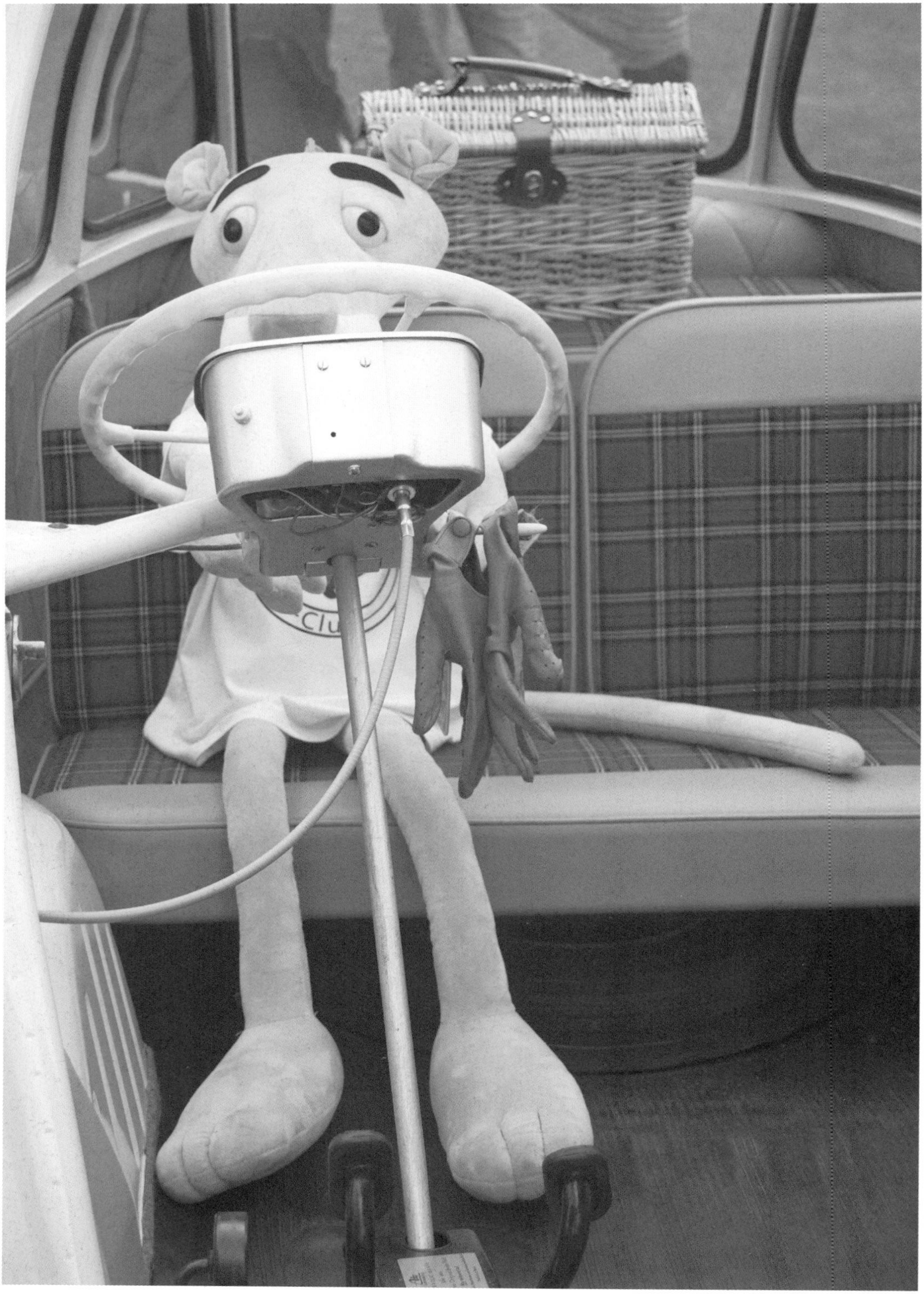

Car owner positions a driver inside their classic car.

Crowds gather around the attractions.

An enthusiast admires the cars on show.

Ford Anglia exhibit.

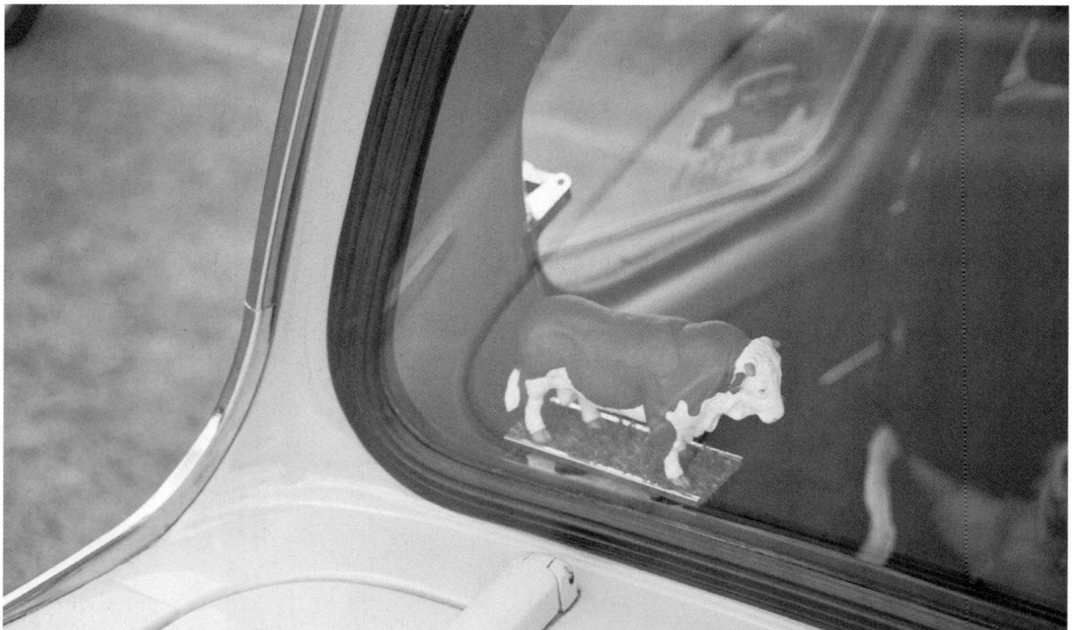

An ornament decorates a rear window.

Sightseers browse the rows of classic vehicles.

An amusing window sticker.

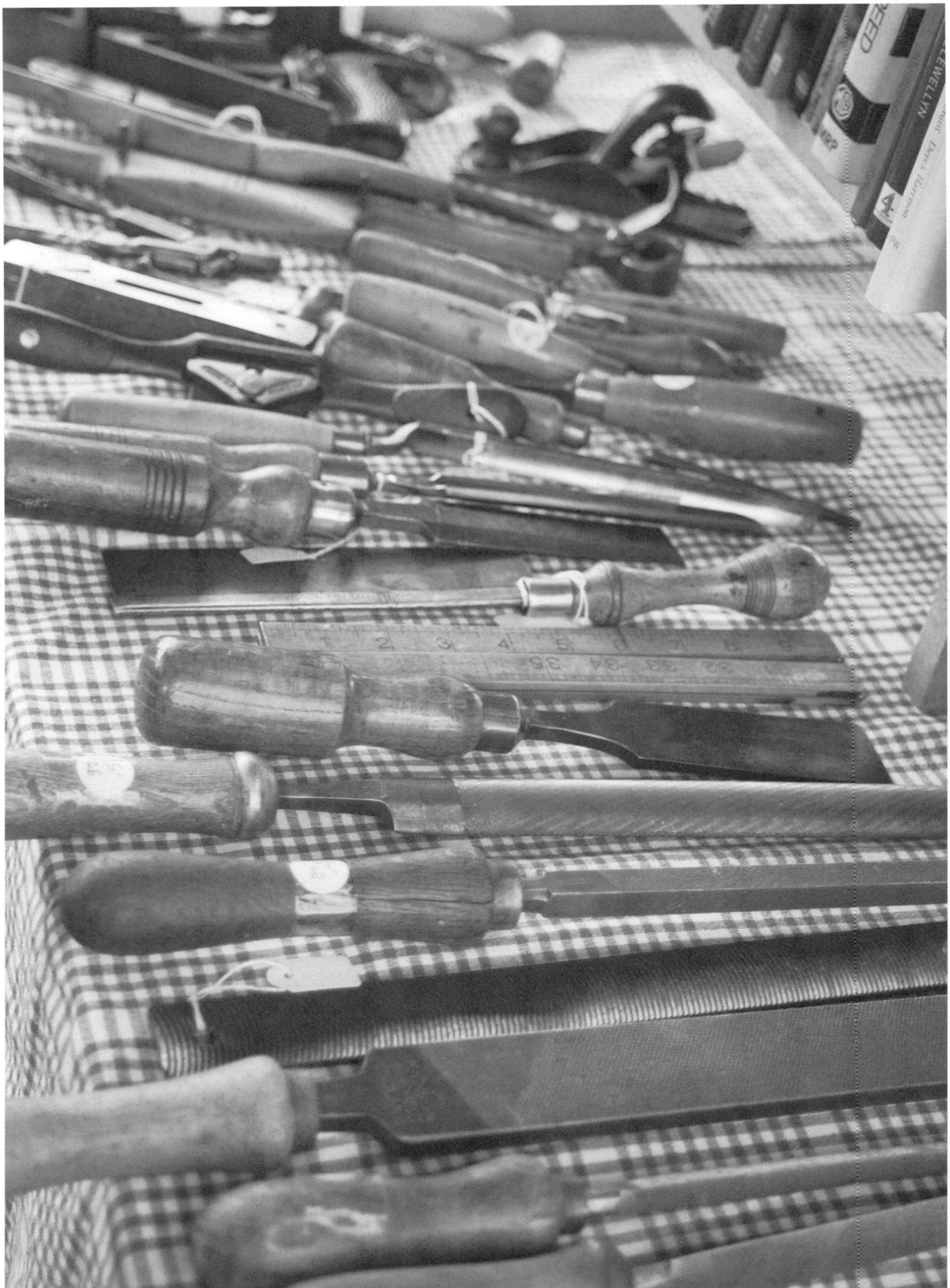

A range of old tools available to buy.

An unwanted bike and collection of retro tins for purchase.

A humorous choice of T-shirt for a show day.

Four

Winchcombe Country Show, Monday 29 August

Winchcombe is an ancient Anglo-Saxon town situated in the Cotswold valley between Broadway and Cheltenham. Every summer the scenic location is home to the Winchcombe Country Show, where residents celebrate their community, kicking off the day with a village procession made up of floats, costumes, dancers and vehicles. The show opens once the parade reaches the show site and a full day of competitions, performances and attractions commences.

One major event is the flower show, which held its 67th annual show in 2016. Various classes are open for entry and certificates, cups and monetary prizes are handed out to lucky winners. Classes include photography, vegetables, fruit, preserves, cookery, art and wine, as well as junior classes for children.

Over the years, Winchcombe has had many themes for its show and 2016's procession focused on the 2016 Rio Olympics. Another theme throughout the day was the Queen's birthday, with numerous exhibits celebrating Her Royal Highness's ninetieth.

The show attracts many villagers from in and around the Cotswolds and raises money for Gloucestershire charities. This includes donations to Winchcombe Fire and Rescue, four local schools, the Butterfly Garden Charity, and Winchcombe Young Farmers.

The day's events.

Cyclists ride through the village as part of the procession.

Residents watch the parade go through the street.

A tractor pulls a trailer of villagers in line with the parade.

An old tractor leads the vintage vehicles.

Local homemade preserves.

Woodcrafter demonstrates his workmanship.

Basket-weaving tools and materials.

A basket-weaver shows her traditional techniques.

Vintage ice-cream truck.

A packed audience watches the dog events.

A busy show site draws in local people.

Judge assigns cups to the prizeworthy winners.

A vegetable box exhibit in the produce tent.

Royal-themed flowers take first prize.

Flower arrangement celebrating the Queen's 90th birthday.

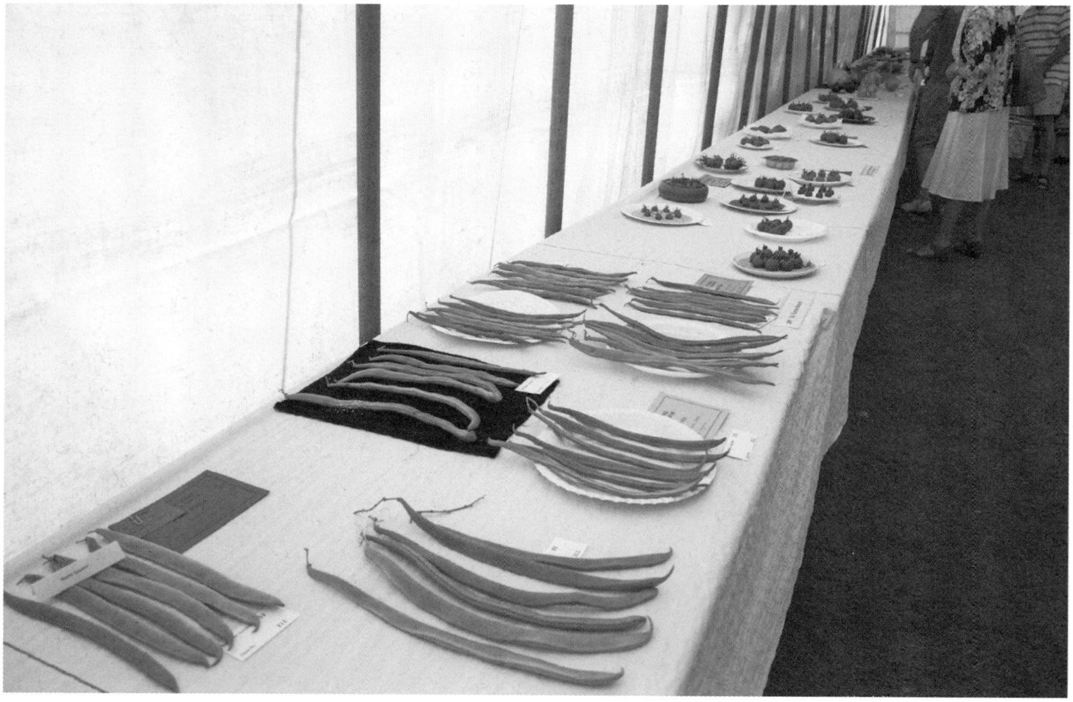

Entries in the green bean class.

Exhibitor wins first prize with chillies.

Inside the competition tent.

Homebrew exhibits.

Show programmes.

Cups and prizes are handed out to lucky winners.

Food vehicles feed the show-goers.

Morris dancers play their customary music.

Morris dancers perform in their costumes.

Dogs take part in the amateur dog show.

Various dog breeds enter the assorted canine classes.

Dog enjoys a day at the show.

Families experience the festival atmosphere.

Surrounding areas of the Cotswolds.

Five

Moreton in Marsh Show, Saturday 3 September

Moreton Show is one of the country's biggest single-day agricultural and horse shows. The first event was held in 1949 on part of the Batsford estate and, since then, the show has run each year at the same site. Moreton Show is split into zones; visitors can look around areas dedicated to home and garden, the countryside, livestock, food, retail, rural attractions, family fun and equine. Around 350 trade stands sell food, drink, gifts and clothing and crowds gather around the grand arena to be entertained.

Friendly rivalry and anticipation fills the busy and excited show atmosphere when rural communities go head to head in farming and equine competitions. In 2016, judges awarded breeders and handlers for their influence on livestock and gave rosettes to the best cattle, sheep, poultry and goats within their breed classes. Industry organisations also attend the show each summer and offer advice, services and demonstrations. The Game and Wildlife Conservation Trust, Agricology, and the National Farmers' Union are just a few significant businesses that can be found in the many marquees across the showground.

Like most country shows, Moreton Show encourages interaction between children, adults, animals and the countryside. It brings together those that work in rural industries and those communities that benefit from agriculture, educating, inspiring and preserving traditions.

Sign directs visitors to the show's areas.

Judges make their decisions in the Homes and Gardens Tent.

Browsers shop around the flower stands.

An organised trouser shop advertises luxury country clothing.

Countryside outlets sell tartan attire.

Stacked flat caps arranged in a retail tent.

Luxury baskets for sale.

The rain doesn't deter the public from attending the show.

Products from Gloucestershire are promoted.

Vintage tractor collection.

The Food Hall includes an array of different traders.

Different sellers promote their products on stands.

Showground warning.

A dog sees the sights from its owner's backpack.

Young boy interacts with a calf.

A farmer leaves his equipment behind while taking a break from showing.

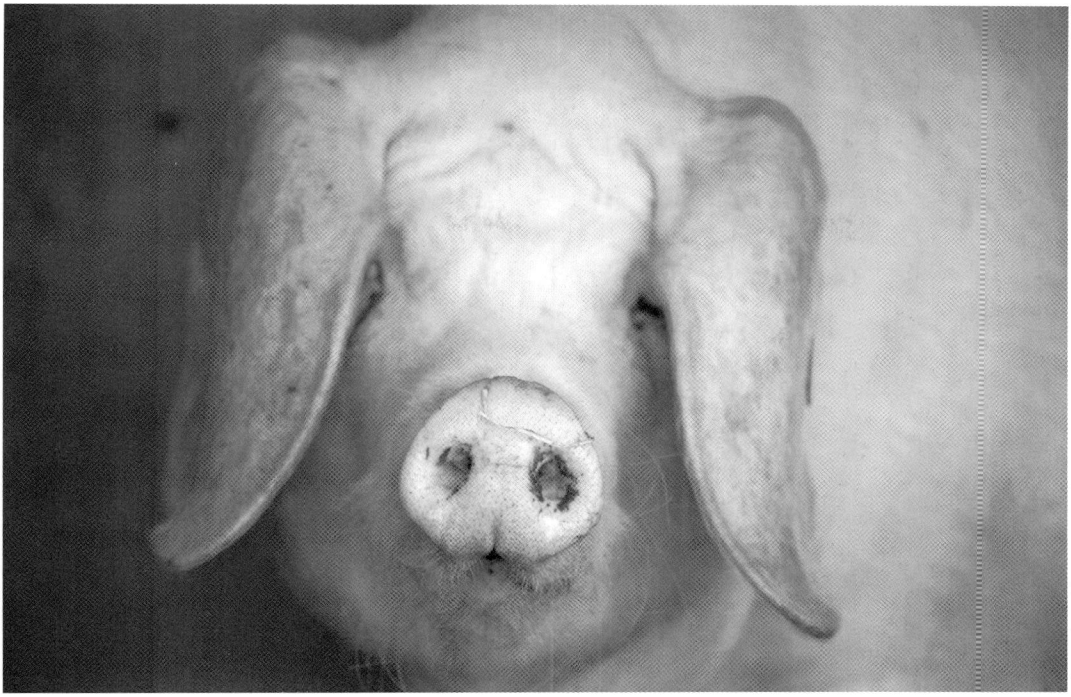

Show pig.

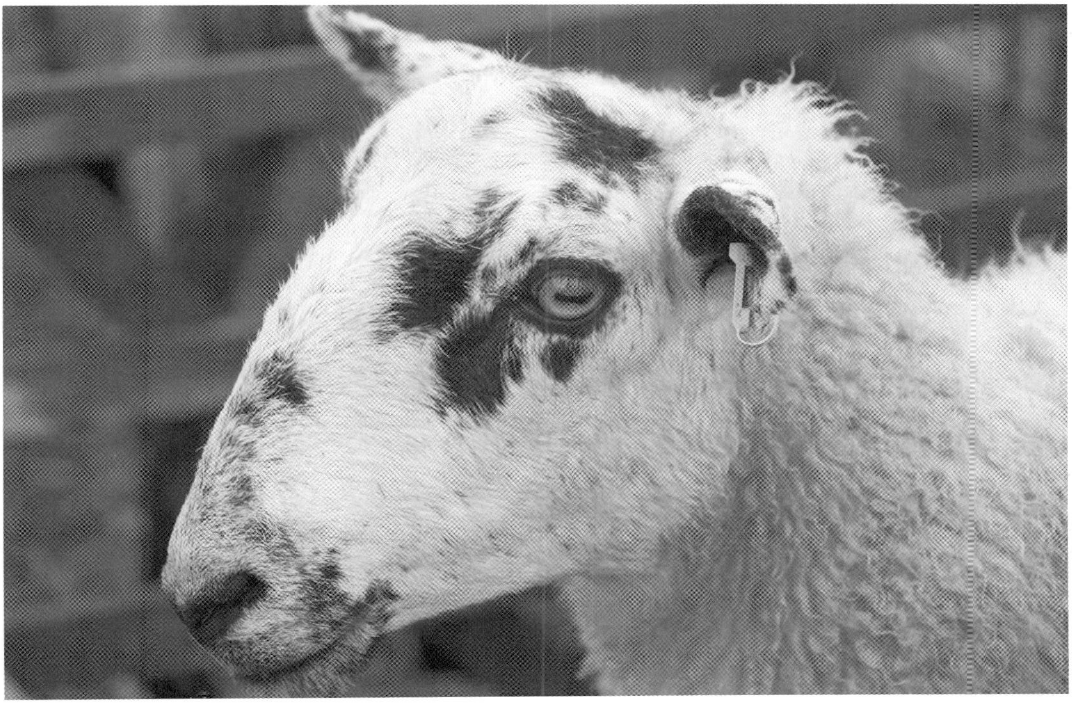

Show sheep.

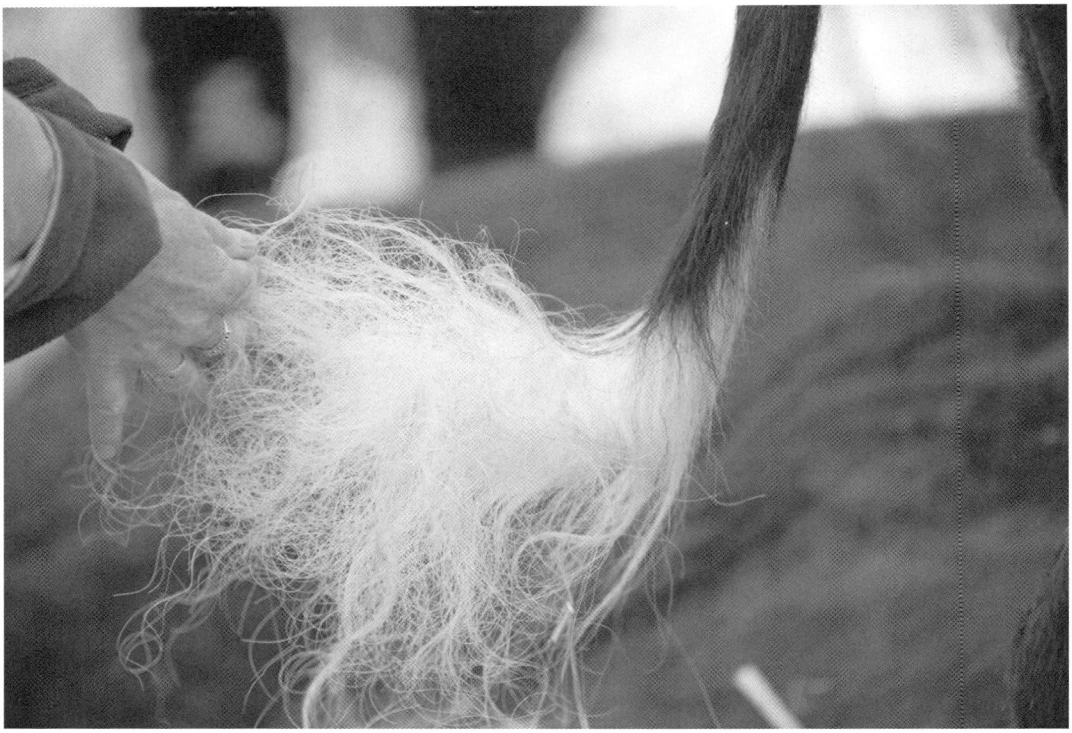

Woman backcombs her cow's tail for judging.

Young piglet.

Instructions left for visitors.

Inquisitive dog and his owner.

Handler controls his show sheep.

A child's novelty vegetable exhibit.

Drinks as well as food are entered into the competition.

Growers display their homegrown produce.

Inside one of the white show tents.

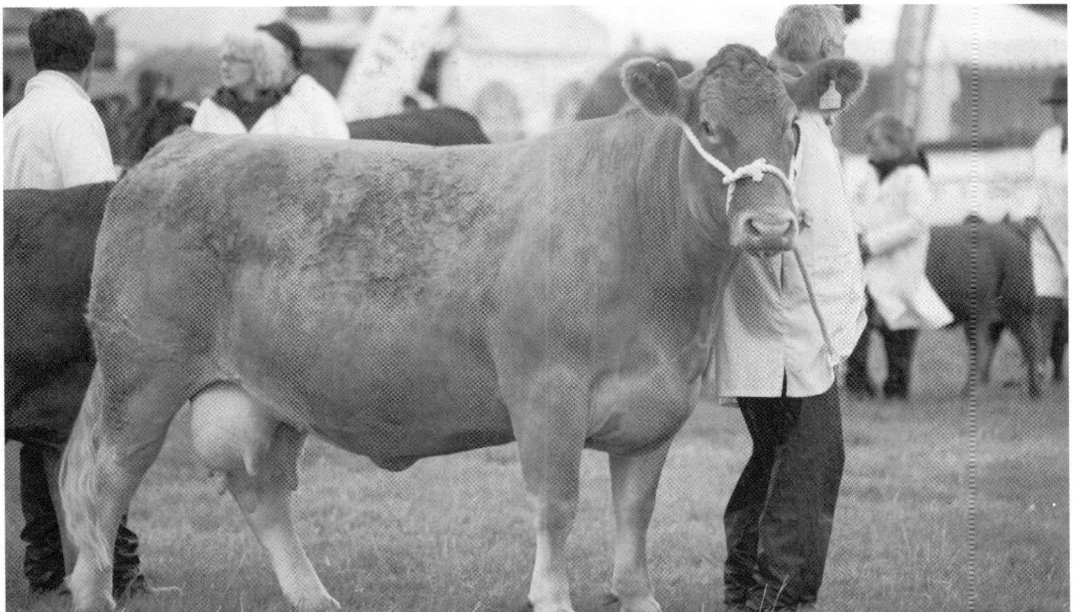

A groomed cow ready for showing.

A young handler walks his sheep around the ring.

Farmer holds his sheep's head for judging.

Six

Frampton Country Fair, Sunday 11 September

Frampton Country Fair was founded by the Gloucestershire Wildfowlers Association in the grounds of Frampton Court Estate – home of the Clifford family. The inaugural event was held in 1986 and celebrated all those that lived and worked in the countryside, and over the years the show has adopted the tagline 'The Living Working Countryside'.

2016 saw the thirty-first fair commence at its home in Frampton Court. The estate has been in the Clifford family since the eleventh century and possesses 1,500 acres of mixed farmland, lakes, woodland and wetland. Utilising this wonderful location, the fair's attractions include dog agility, ferret racing, shooting, fishing and horsemanship to name but a few. Unlike other country shows, Frampton also features more unusual events including an elver eating competition and a bale push, where teams must move a silage bale around an obstacle course three-legged!

The huge array of things to see and do at Frampton Country Fair attracts thousands of people, and 2016's show was full of visitors taking up the opportunity to see traditional skills, industries and professions all in one place. The rural skills tent held demonstrations on knot tying, stick making, spinning and basket making and there was even a mobile milking parlour and vintage cider press on display.

Fairground amusements.

A drystone walling demonstration.

Woman carries a tired collie puppy in her bag.

Onlookers watch Main Ring events.

Working vintage dairy display.

Clown mixes with the people.

Gundog training display.

The Gloucestershire Wildfowlers Association organise rural activities.

Equine sports run throughout the day.

Large crowds enjoy the sunshine on a Sunday afternoon.

A dog swims back to his owner in a retrieval exercise.

Show entertainer Professor Crump wanders the showground greeting guests.

Fly-casting demonstration.

The hunt gather their hounds and horses in the paddock.

Huntsman blows a hunting horn and calls the hounds.

Cavalry member prepares for the Tent Pegging demonstration.

Pet owners control their dogs to take part in competitions.

A dog finishes the Scramble, a race where both handlers and dogs complete timed obstacles.

People buy show guides to plan their day.

A mass parade of hounds are welcomed into the Main Arena.

A traditional historic cider press in use.

The Wye Valley Axemen race against each other using razor-sharp saws and lumberjack techniques.

Seven

Cotswold Living Landscape Festival, Sunday 18 September

The very first Cotswold Living Landscape Festival was held on a sunny Sunday in 2016 to mark the fiftieth anniversary of the Cotswold Area of Outstanding Natural Beauty. Organised by the Cotswold Conservation Board, the festival was located at the beautiful Lodge Park on National Trust's Sherbourne estate.

The Cotswolds is one of the largest protected landscapes in England and the festival celebrated everything that makes the place so special. The show focused on native art, regional animals, historic rural skills, local food and wildlife. The Cotswold sheep breed were on view, there was a drystone walling competition and wood carving, sheep dog trials and horse logging demonstrations. Stage performances included big band and folk music, Morris dancers and instrumentalists. Guided walks took visitors around the surrounding areas, and both bike and minibus tours encouraged people to explore the local landscape. The Lodge Park building was open to the public throughout the day and families looked out over the showground from the impressive building, which was created in 1634.

Entrance to the festival.

Wood sculptor at work.

Lodge Park.

Areas of the showground.

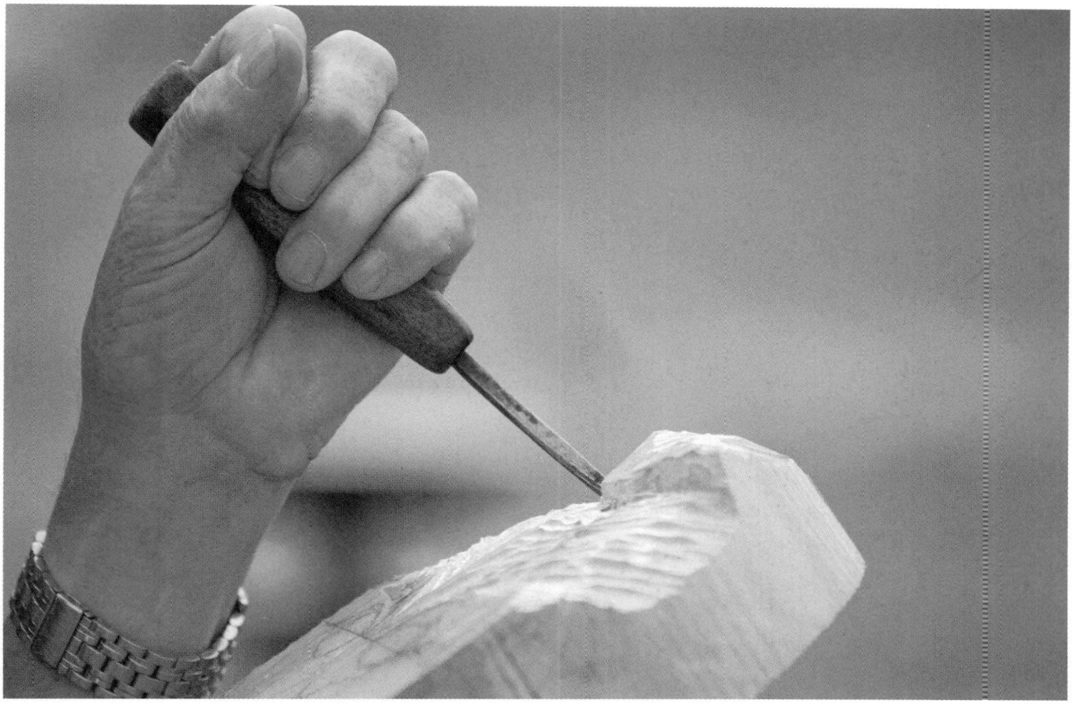

Woodcarver creates owl design.

A bear chiselled into timber.

View through Lodge Park balcony.

Showground from above.

Visitor exits Lodge Park to return to the show's events.

England's only surviving seventeenth-century grandstand.

A classic ice-cream van.

A man shapes stone to build his wall.

A Cotswold sheep.

Native sheep breed at the show.

Horse lorry.

Competitors participate in a drystone walling contest.

Craftsman creates a wooden sculpture.

Families revel in the festival atmosphere.

Musicians sing and play instruments for the crowd.

Morris group dance for the audience.

A Morris Dancer's jacket.

A member of the British Woodcarvers' Association.

Young girls meets an alpaca.

A groomed alpaca.

7 day loan

A HANDBOOK OF

TRAINING MANAGEMENT